Compassionate Laughter:
Jest For Your Health!

What Others Are Saying About *Compassionate Laughter*

Compassionate Laughter is the ultimate resource for people wishing to understand the health benefits of laughter. Besides presenting an accurate description of the scientific research, Wooten provides a comprehensive glossary and extensive literature base. A must for those serious about laughter!

> —Lee S. Berk, DrPH, MPH, FACSM, Assistant Professor of Health Promotion and Education, Schools of Medicine and Public Health, Loma Linda University

Every nurse should read *Compassionate Laughter*. It will strengthen their compassion. I laughed out loud through the whole book!

> –Carol Montgomery, RN, PhD, author of *Healing Through Communication: The Practice of Caring*

As a breast cancer survivor and one who speaks about the importance of humor and healing to cancer survivors and those who care for them, this is a must-read book! It will truly benefit us and those we care for.

> —Jane Hill, BS, Comedienne and breast cancer survivor; author of *Keep Laughing to Keep Healthy*

Compassionate Laughter integrates the body, mind and spirit. This is a valuable contribution to the future of healing, for professionals and laypersons alike!

> —Barbara Dossey, RN, MS, FACN, author of *Holistic Nursing: A Handbook for Practice,* and *Cardiovascular Nursing: Body, Mind, Spirit*

Compassionate Laughter will bring fun, excitement, and wonder to any reader! Patty presents valuable information about the benefits of humor and laughter for health, for getting along with other people, and for dealing with the frustrating and sometimes depressing aspects of everyday life. It is full of both wisdom and chuckles!

> —William F. Fry, MD, Professor Emeritus, Stanford University

This is not a dry treatise on humor—it is a book that will touch the soul of the reader who is or has visions of becoming a caring clown. I was moved by this book's message!

> —Richard Snowberg EdD, Assoc. Professor, University of Wisconsin, La Crosse, and *Clown Camp* Director

Humor is as necessary in a caregiver's armamentarium as any physical or medicinal therapies—so read this book and you'll be well-armed!

—I. Martin Grais, MD, FACP, FACC, Assistant Professor of Clinical Medicine, Northwestern University Medical School

Compassionate Laughter is a great resource for health professionals. If this country's health providers would embrace Patty's ideas, health care would heal itself.

—Doug Fletcher, RN, Editor of *Journal of Nursing Jocularity*

This book offers the blueprint for re-energizing and renewing your zest for patient care. Read this book—it will repay your effort a thousand-fold in levity!

—Frank Barry, MD, author of *Make the Change for a Healthy Heart*, Family Physician and Executive Director of Preventive Health Institute

Patty takes readers on a joyful journey that combines passion and compassion with information and inspiration. Read it and reap!

–Allen Klein, author of *The Healing Power of Humor* and *Quotations to Cheer You Up*

What a warm, wonderful book! Patty Wooten has gathered all the resources anyone would need to use laughter in healing. It is essential reading for those who believe laughter is good medicine!

—Vera M. Robinson, RN, EdD, Fairy Godmother of Humor, author of *Humor and the Health Professions*

Compassionate Laughter should be required reading for anyone involved in the healthcare field, from practitioner to patient! Patty offers a thorough and humor-filled master plan for incorporating humor in healthcare services. Looking for a solution to the healthcare crisis? Here's one. No Kidding!

—Irene Sassoon, Stand-Up Comic, and Executive Assistant to Andrew Weil, MD, author of *Spontaneous Healing*

Anyone reading *Compassionate Laughter* will obtain a clear understanding of the physical, emotional and spiritual benefits of laughter. They will also find a wealth of practical ideas for putting humor to work in any health care setting.

—Paul E. McGhee, PhD, author of *How to Develop Your Sense of Humor: Life Skills for Boosting Resilience and Job Performance Under Stress*

Compassionate Laughter: Jest For Your Health!

By
Patty Wooten, R.N.

Commune-A-Key Publishing
Salt Lake City, UT 84158

Commune-A-Key Publishing
P.O. Box 58637
Salt Lake City, UT 84158
1-800-983-0600

Library in Congress Cataloging-in-Publication Data
Wooten, Patty.
    Compassionate laughter: jest for your health / by Patty Wooten.
       p. cm.
Includes bibliographical references and index.
ISBN 1-881394-41-4 (pbk. : alk. paper)
1. Wit and humor—Therapeutic use.
I. Title.
R705.W64 1996   615.8' . 51—dc20
                                   96-13995
                                      CIP

Editorial: Caryn Summers and Nancy Lang
Cover Design: Lightbourne Images, Ashland, OR
Photography: Paul Herzoff, Emeryville, CA
Typeset Design: Bailey-Montague & Associates, Salt Lake City, UT

Table of Contents

Dedication

To those who heal with compassion and laughter.

Acknowledgments

Wow! I really wrote a book! I must have, my name is on the cover! As I wrote, it became clear how many people have blessed my life with their laughter. These people have given me the courage, inspiration, and information to bring this book from idea to reality. Some of these people inspired my intellectual understanding, others inspired my clowning skills. Some kept the home fires burning, others kept the office fires extinguished. All of these people have taught me the truth about Compassionate Laughter. Since I won't be sharing my royalty checks with them, I want to acknowledge and thank them for helping me. They deserve Oscars for the Best Performances in a Creative Role. Here are the winners!

Best Producers:
Mom and Dad! My deepest gratitude to my parents, Yvonne and Richard Savercool. They showed me the value of laughter. After fifty years, they still laugh together everyday.

Best Actors:
Ken Wooten, my son, who brings me more joy than anyone in my life. Thanks for all the research on Native American clowns. I admit I was wrong about how practical your degree in anthropology would be!

Deak Wooten, my friend, husband, father of my child, ex-husband and now, my friend again. Thanks for hanging around until we could laugh together again!

Rick Savercool, my brother, who taught me to throw a baseball faster than any girl in the fifth grade, and then laughed when I knocked over Dad's prized Bonsai tree.

Best Choreographer:
Christi Bengard, my dearest friend and advisor. Thanks for your idea to create Nurse Kindheart and for helping me bring her to life. Best of all, thanks for encouraging me to play.

Best Dog:
Becky, my playful Airedale pup, thanks for your devotion and warm nuzzles.

Best Director:
Caryn Summers, my publisher, and Nancy Lang, my editor, thanks for your words of wisdom, encouragement and direction through the difficult moments. Your keen eyes, attention to detail and demand for excellence was exhausting, but I am proud of what we have created together. I could not have done this without you.

Best Technical Assistance:
Wendy Miller-Easton, my secretary and Lois Richter, my research assistant: thanks for helping me gather and organize the volumes of information necessary for this book, and for keeping my business organized when I ran away to write.

Best Actresses:
Thanks to my dear friends, Rosemarie Delahaye, Muriel Heritage, Suzanne Sandige, Binnie Hart, Jane Lloyd and Mary Caroline, who have been helping me laugh through many difficult moments since 1964.

Best Artistic Creation:
Thanks to my photographer, Paul Herzoff and cover designers Gaelyn and Bram Larrick, for capturing the heart and message of this book with your artistic images. I hope everyone will judge this book by its cover! Thanks to John Wise, Bob Quick, Tom Jackson, and Brian Moench, talented cartoonists with an ability to capture the bizarre and funny side of health care humor.

Best Inspiration:
Thanks to Bill Fry, Vera Robinson, Lee Berk, Stanley Tan, Norman Cousins, Doug Fletcher and Michael Christiansen. Your courage and vision made the road easier for all of us who have followed your example. You have inspired and guided my work.

Best Actresses in a Supporting Role:

Thanks to my collegues and humor buddies: Karyn Buxman, Sandy Ritz, Fran London, Dixie Schneider, Leslie Gibson, Donna Strickland, Carol Montgomery, Jane Hill, Jan Adrian, Karen Lee and Polly Schack. Your advice and encouragement have been essential in creating this book.

Best Actors in a Supporting Role:

Thanks to my humor pals and fellow humor speakers: Allen Klein, Christian Hageseth, Terry Paulsen, Jim Pelley, Bruce Stombach, Joe Dunn, Martin Grais and Cliff Kuhn. You have inspired me to grow and improve in the art of communication.

Best Spiritual Advisor:

God, Director of Heaven and Earth. Thank you for being there every time I asked for help, and for coming along anyway, when I didn't think I needed you.

Best Assistants to the Spiritual Advisor:

Jack Kornfield, Barbara Dossey, Larry Dossey and Cal Samra. Thanks for helping me understand and share the essence of spirit in humor.

Best Clown Advisors:

Arina Isaacson, Kenny Ahern, Cathy Gibbons, Richard Snowberg, Wavy Gravy, Bonnie Donaldson, Janet Tucker, Steve Kissell and Roly Bain. Thanks for being my mentors, 'foolish' advisors, and for your compassionate clowning.

Best Comedy Artists

Lily Tomlin, thanks for showing me the incredible power of character based comedy. Thank you for 'Edith Ann,' my personal favorite. Robin Williams, thanks for your zany, quick-witted comedy and wonderful voice impersonations. Thanks for Mrs. Doubtfire, who is "Nurse Kindheart's" idol, mentor and inspiration. And finally, to Dimitri the Clown, thanks for showing me the joyful innocence of a clown's heart.

Prologue

You are about to begin an exciting journey into the world of therapeutic humor, and I hope you have as much fun as I have had in creating this path for you to travel. As I gathered and reviewed the information and stories for this book, I had many opportunities to laugh. I also had many opportunities to sweat! One author described writing as easy, "You just sit down with a pen and paper and wait until blood drips from your forehead." As a professional speaker, I no longer suffer from stage fright, but writing this book has provided moments of "keyboard fright" that made me sweat!

After 25 years as a nurse, 20 years as a clown, and 10 years as a humor speaker, I knew there was a book inside of me. I was just too busy to sit down and write it. One day, Nurse-Publisher Caryn Summers approached me at a conference where we were both speaking. She asked me to write a book about compassionate laughter. I knew that one of the most difficult factors in becoming an author was to find an interested publisher. I eagerly signed the contract.

Then I learned about the other difficult factor in becoming an author—the ability to communicate with clarity, conviction and reader comfort. What flowed easily through me on stage became awkward as I faced the computer screen. I had to learn how to write. Now, for someone who took bonehead English in college, this lesson was an uphill journey! Fortunately, both Caryn and my editor, Nancy Lang, guided and encouraged me. My family, friends and humor buddies, as you will read in the acknowledgments, all played an important part in helping me bring this book to life.

During nursing school, when I got tired or frustrated, I encouraged myself by saying, "If I am able to save just one life or ease just one person's suffering, then all the struggle will be worth it." Now, 25 years later after writing this book, I offer a similar statement, "If I can help just one person to laugh or find their inner jester, then all the struggle will be worth it."

Introduction

Here I lie, I have a tumor . . .
and you ask me where's my sense of humor?

—David Saltzman

In his senior year at Yale David Saltzman was diagnosed with Hodgkin's Disease, a cancer of the lymphatic system. Upon hearing the news, he went out to a patch of lawn, sat by a tree and cried. After listening to his own sobs, thinking how much they sounded like his laughter, he remembered a line he had written the previous summer: "Here I lie, I have a tumor . . . and you ask me where's my sense of humor?" At that moment, his inner Jester put a hand on his shoulder and said, "David, how come you're not laughing? Your cries sound just like laughs, so why not laugh instead?" David thought about it, got up from the pile of dead leaves that surrounded him, wiped his face dry of tears, and walked off laughing at how silly, scary and wonderful this world can be.

David died a few weeks before his 23rd birthday; however, until those final moments, he served as an inspiration for those facing difficult situations. David knew how to laugh, and he knew how essential laughter was when facing a serious illness. Before he died, David completed a delightful book, *The Jester Has Lost His Jingle,* a story about a Jester who brings laughter back to his kingdom.

Do you hear the sweet sound of laughter in your kingdom, either at work or at home? Are you caring for someone who has lost the jingle of their inner Jester? Perhaps *you* have forgotten how to laugh. Does your inner Jester need a wake up call? Are you ready to bring laughter back into your life and into the lives of those you love and care for? This book will help—it is a guide, textbook, and storybook all rolled into one. It is designed to bring *you* face to face with your inner Jester. It is designed to bring laughter back into your kingdom.

Laughter is Good for You

There is no doubt that laughter is *good* for you. But, *how good* is it for you? And, *how* is it good is it for you? A hearty laugh feels great! At that magical moment of laughter, we feel relaxed, hopeful, open and forgiving. We no longer feel anxious, hostile, depressed, or alone.

A sense of humor helps us recognize and appreciate the comedic potential of any situation. This "comic vision" enables us to see both the serious and the absurd possibilities of any circumstance. At that comic moment, our feelings shift to amusement or surprise and stimulate laughter. This book provides convincing evidence that mirthful laughter is powerful medicine for our body, mind and spirit.

What Makes Us Laugh?

"I Love Lucy" made people laugh for many years. In one episode, Lucy and Ethel are working in a candy factory, placing candies from a conveyor belt into candy boxes. Their supervisor notices how well this process is going and turns up the speed on the belt. Lucy and Ethel move faster to get the candies into the boxes before they fall onto the floor. They begin eating a few candies, and the audience laughs. Again, the supervisor notices how well things are going and increases the conveyor speed. Lucy and Ethel work frantically to keep up. They are forced to eat even more candy and begin stuffing them in their pockets. The audience laughs even harder as they see Lucy and Ethel's facial expressions and their comical movements. Again and again, the conveyor speed is increased until the audience is in tears, roaring with laughter. They rock back and forth in their seats, slapping their knees. Tears flow freely. The audience is left breathless and gasping, yet their eyes are twinkling with delight and their bodies are relaxed. Strange behavior. Why do we laugh? Chapter 1 will help you understand how comical situations, like Lucy in the candy factory, stimulates laughter and brings feelings of joy.

Learning to Laugh at Yourself and Your Situation

Are you able to laugh at yourself? Can you find some humor in a situation or illness you may be facing? Some of the patients I cared for showed me that this was possible. Many years ago, I attended nursing school in San Francisco. Market Street is a main route running through the City, from the hilltops down to Fisherman's Wharf. As I prepared my patient, Mrs. Dodge, for her third abdominal surgery, I noticed a long scar running the length of her torso. She noticed my surprise and announced that she called it "Market Street," because it went from Twin Peaks (her breasts) all the way down to the waterfront (her pubic area). I learned then, how some patients used humor to help them cope with the often disfiguring changes that result from medical treatments. This book will help you develop skills to find a humorous perspective, to use "comic vision" to look beyond your immediate circumstances, and, to continue to enjoy all the areas of your life!

Sensitivity With Humor

Have you ever experienced humor that left you feeling alone or confused? Not all types of humor and comedy make us feel better. It is important to understand that humor has the power to create both positive and negative reactions. If we use humor as one of our caregiving tools, we must choose humor that builds connections and expresses understanding. We must be sensitive to the culture, gender, and boundaries of those we hope to amuse. Sarcasm, racist, or put down humor feeds anger and bitterness, and creates a sense of separation from others. Even some types of humor that caregivers find amusing may be offensive to the care receivers. Chapter 2 shows you how to use humor to express your compassion and improve your caregiving skills. You will also learn how it can protect you, the caregiver, from the stress of providing care.

Humor in the Hospital

Throughout my years of nursing I have met many patients who were able to call upon their inner jester in times of stress. One such example was Mr. Barnes. He was scheduled for abdominal surgery and he was anxious, scared of the unknown, the pain, and especially of the strangers who would be invading his body. Perhaps, he thought, if he could feel a connection with those strangers in masks, he could relax and feel safe. A friend visited the night before surgery and provided the solution. The next morning, Mr. Barnes arrived in the operating room grinning from ear to ear. After the staff began preparing him for surgery, they started to laugh. Placed on his belly, they found a sticker requesting, "Hey, Doc . . . while you're in there could you check the oil?" The staff congratulated Mr. Barnes on his delightful joke and they all eagerly awaited the arrival of the surgeon, who quickly joined in the laughter. Immediately, everyone felt a sense of relaxation and camaraderie as they laughed together and shared this comic moment. As Mr. Barnes drifted into sleep, he knew he was among friends.

Moments of playfulness and shared laughter bring people closer together and can change our attitude about a difficult situation. The language of laughter expresses our understanding, our compassion, and allows us to connect as equals, spirit to spirit, in an intimate way. As for Mr. Barnes, after the surgeon completed his surgery, he placed a strip of tape on the bed with these words, "Oil checked, tires rotated, next inspection tomorrow morning or 30,000 miles, whichever comes first!"

Laughter as Medicine

For centuries it has been proclaimed that "Laughter is the best medicine." In psychology, in spiritual teachings, in anthropological recordings, in literature and now, finally in scientific and medical journals, we are proving that, "A merry heart doeth good like a medicine."

Norman Cousins in his book, *Anatomy of an Illness*, describes how he successfully used laughter to facilitate his recovery from a serious illness. Cousins' inspired the scientific community to look closely at the effect of laughter on our body. Some of the most interesting results have come from the field of psychoneuroimmunology (PNI). PNI explores the link between the brain and the immune system, and attempts to answer the question, "Do our thoughts and emotions create changes in our body?" Published research about the mind-body connection has increased dramatically in the last ten years. In Chapter 3, these connections are defined and the scientific evidence that laughter stimulates healthy changes in our bodies is reviewed.

Humor Therapy Programs

Successful humor therapy programs in hospitals, nursing homes, medical offices and home care agencies are providing mirthful medicine. For many people, the hospital is a frightening place. Patients and their visitors expect a somber environment filled with serious professionals and impersonal technology. How often have you heard the sounds of laughter spilling into the hallways of hospitals? In many hospitals this "dearth of mirth" is disappearing.

In New York City, clowns from the Big Apple Circus-Clown Care Unit visit patients and their families every day. In the 1970's, DeKalb Hospital in Decatur, Georgia created one of the first Therapeutic Humor Rooms. There are now hundreds of similar rooms in hospitals across the country. Nurse Leslie Gibson created a Comedy Cart to provide a mobile unit to deliver "humor on call" to patients at the Morton Plant Hospital in Clearwater, Florida. Cathy Johnson, a nurse at Dartmouth Hitchcock Medical Center in New Hampshire, assembled a Humor Basket of toys and props to provide a playful diversion for patients and staff. We may all agree that humor should be added to treatment regimes, but it may be awkward to know how to get started. In Chapter 4, you will be introduced to a wide variety of successful humor programs. You will learn what they are doing and how they are doing it. Guidelines, suggestions and resources will help you create a humor program in your home or hospital.

The Laughing Spirit

Do you suffer from terminal seriousness? Are you convinced that you could never develop the skills to find humor in your situation? Do not despair! You can still experience laughter by allowing other humorists to give you that "comic vision." As you are developing your humor skills, don't wait to enjoy the laughter. If you know *what* to look for and *where* to look for it, you can find plenty of comedy in books, films, audio programs, videotapes, cartoons and even on the Internet. Throughout this book, we will present examples of different styles of humor. However, just as taste preferences for food vary from person to person, so will your taste vary for humor. You have to sample and decide what tickles your funny bone. We have included hundreds of resources where you may obtain humor supplies that will develop your humor skills.

Why You Should Read This Book

Life is serious. Death is serious. Illness is serious. Newspapers and TV reports continually remind us of how serious everything is. The government and our bosses tell us how serious things are. We become worried, frightened, angry and discouraged. Our bodies are listening to this emotional weather report. Gradually, and sometimes suddenly, cells within our body change behavior and start to carry messages advising us to make adjustments so that we may protect ourselves. If our bodies are continually forced to change and adjust to negative emotions, we may become sick. Humor and laughter provide the relief that protects our body.

Whether you are looking for an understanding of the form and function of humor; for scientific evidence of laughter's healing potential; or for guidelines to establish a therapeutic humor program for your family or facility, *Compassionate Laughter* will give you ideas and answers. So, settle back, chuckle-up, and get ready to explore the healing Heart of Humor!

Chapter 1
The Laughing Heart

Laughter is a melody, a concert from the heart,
a tickling by the angels, creative living art.
Laughter heals and comforts, sometimes gentle, sometimes bold.
Laughter is a freeing dance, performed within the soul.
—Serene West

The Heart of Humor

Humor is a complex phenomena that is an essential part of human nature. Throughout the ages, anthropologists have never found a culture or society that was devoid of humor. We humans begin to smile and laugh during the first few months of life. Even animals display signs of playfulness and humor during their development. Unless our body, mind, or spirit is severely damaged, we will continue to laugh until the moment of our death.

On his death bed, American humorist Oscar Wilde,
looked about his room and informed his friend,
"This wall paper is awful. One of us has to go!"

A sense of humor is both a perspective on life—a way of perceiving the world—and a behavior that expresses that perspective. To experience the joy that humor can bring, we must share in the laughter with others. If we want to improve our sense of humor, we must learn to look for the absurdity in every moment. One such moment stands out clearly in my memory....

Most of my nursing experience has been in Intensive Care Units, caring for critically ill patients. I will always remember Ruth, and the moments we spent laughing together. Ruth had Chronic Obstructive Pulmonary Disease (COPD). Her lungs were severely damaged from the chemical fumes she had inhaled during a lifetime of factory work. They were so deteriorated that they could no longer absorb enough oxygen to keep her alive. We had cared for her for almost three weeks. Despite increasing levels of oxygen flow, her blood gases continued to decline and she finally required ventilator support. I had cared for her for five consecutive days, and during that period we'd grown very close. I had consoled her grieving husband, calmed her worried adult children, and provided as much comfort and dignity for Ruth as I could. I was exhausted and eagerly anticipated my three days off.

Ruth's condition was so poor, I was certain she would not survive more than one or two days. If I wanted to say good-bye to her, I knew I must do it before I left that day. Near the end of my shift, I stood at her bedside trying to find the words to express how much I admired her courage, and of how much she had taught me about love and kindness. I shared that I would miss her if she died before I returned from my days off. As I stumbled to express these painful emotions, tears began to flow from my eyes. I was soon too choked up with emotion to continue.

Ruth reached up to pat my forearm and smiled. At that moment, I saw the absurdity of the moment: she, the terminally ill patient was comforting the supposedly strong and competent professional. I began to laugh, saying, "Look at us! I'm an emotional wreck and you're taking care of me! That's a real switch." She smiled, nodded her head and laughed. In that moment of ridiculous incongruity, we connected at a deep and spiritual level. I learned just how powerful humor can be in connecting two people.

It Begins With a Smile

A smile is a child's first language, and eager parents are often rewarded with one in the first six weeks of life. A smile gains attention, invites interaction, and expresses understanding. A baby's smile has a magnetic attraction that engages us immediately. Watch any adult in the presence of a smiling baby—they make strange noises, contort their face into comical expressions and generally make a fool of themselves, just to see that baby smile one more time (Lewis, 1987).

Laughter is a smile that engages the entire body. At first, the corners of the mouth turn up slightly, then the muscles around your eyes engage and a twinkling in the eyes appears. Next you begin to make noises, ranging from controlled snickers, escaped chortles, and spontaneous giggles, to ridiculous cackles, noisy hoots, and up-roarious guffaws. Your chest and abdominal muscles become activated. As the noises get louder, you begin to bend your body back and forth, sometimes slapping your knees, stomping your feet on the floor or perhaps elbowing another person nearby. As laughter reaches its peak, tears flow freely. All of this continues until you feel so weak and exhausted that you must sit down or fall down. Very strange behavior!

Of course, not everyone experiences such intense laughter every time they are amused. If we are concerned about how others might judge this behavior; if we are concerned with maintaining a dignified image; if we feel others might be offended by our robust laughter; or if our culture places strong taboos on such behavior, then we may struggle to contain ourselves. Bankers and funeral directors usually do not exhibit this robust laughter on the job. During a church service or hospital crisis, we may subdue or postpone our laughter. Women in Asian and Middle Eastern cultures are usually expected to refrain from robust, unrestrained laughter in public social circles. But, when you're in the mood and feeling free-spirited, let go, stomp your feet, slap your knees, and let loose with an uproarious guffaw!!

Despite its outlandish appearance, laughter provides important psychological benefits. It serves as an inner safety valve that allows us to release tension, dispel worry, relax and let go. Inside everyone is a laughing spirit!

Where Does Humor Come From?

The basic foundation for a sense of humor is a spirit of playfulness (McGhee, 1994). We can access our playfulness by acting silly. The word "silly" is derived from two old European words, "Seely" and "Saelig," both of which mean happy, joyful and blessed. Elephant jokes are a form of verbal silliness that provide nothing other than the sheer joy of nonsense. For example:

> Q: How does an elephant hide?
> A: She paints her toenails red and
>   climbs into a cherry tree!

Silly people are spontaneous and playful with everything in their environment.

I remember meeting Dr. Patch Adams for the first time at the International Clown Congress in Philadelphia. Patch describes himself as, 'a silly person and a nutty doctor.' We were attending a luncheon to honor clowns who served their communities. No one was "in face" (in costume) and the atmosphere was one of subdued celebration. At one point during lunch, I looked across the table to where Patch sat, and laughed out loud. He had taken the paper covers off the butter pats and decorated his face with them! Silly behavior is much riskier than sharing 'prepared' humor because it is spontaneous and uninhibited. Silliness might scare or annoy people who are uncomfortable with surprises or feeling out of control. But silliness can be contagious! Help someone around you feel comfortable with laughing and being spontaneous!!

The Power of Playfulness

Watch children play and you will see them using their imagination to invent a reality that meets their needs. If we allow ourselves to be kids and distort or exaggerate a situation to it's most absurd limits, we create an opportunity for laughter. About ten years ago, I worked in the Intensive Care Unit in a small community hospital. A young doctor came on staff after he finished his residency at a large research medical center. Many of the exotic blood tests he ordered were so obscure they were performed only in large medical centers. Making arrangements for these tests created tremendous stress for our laboratory staff because the blood had to be shipped by courier to San Francisco. The lab staff frequently complained to the nurses about this frustration.

One evening we decided to give the lab technicians some "comic relief." We called down and announced that Dr. Stark had just ordered another test. The lab tech groaned and asked which rare test was ordered this time. We tried to act serious, and told him the test was for a "stool velocity," expecting that he would get the joke. But, instead, he believed us and complained that they had no experience with this procedure. We calmly assured him that we had looked it up in the procedure manual, which stated that one tech was to go outside with a specimen cup and the other was to hang the patient's bottom out the upstairs window. They were to measure the time it took for the stool to reach the cup. For the next few months, the lab staff would laugh and ask if there were any orders for a "stool velocity!"

This story demonstrates how our sense of humor helps us to recognize the absurdity in situations of tension, frustration and tragedy. A sense of humor allows us to relieve our tensions with laughter.

How to Develop Humor

Humor is a skill that can be developed. We can begin to perceive, create, and respond to moments of absurdity. Dr. Paul McGhee is an outrageously funny person. But, he wasn't always like that. As a Professor of Developmental Psychology, he was caught up in the seriousness of academia and research. Ironically, his research examined the development of humor in small children. After publishing several serious books about humor, the Professor learned an important lesson from the children he studied: they taught him how to play.

Now, Paul is playful wherever he is. One of his favorite activities is to wear funny noses and glasses while he's driving his car. (My favorite is his horn-rimmed glasses with a long elephant trunk nose!) Paul let his white hair grow long and bushy so that it sticks out around his head and looks like a wild clown wig. He uses his long and lean body to move comically, striking unusual poses. Needless to say, he is no longer in academia, and now devotes his time to helping adults regain their sense of humor and playfulness. His book, *How to Develop Your Sense of Humor,* is one of the best resources on this subject that I have found.

How to Find Humor

To discover the comic potential in a situation, you need to first see the situation, then recognize it, and then accept it. Gene Perret, in his book, *How to Write and Sell Your Sense of Humor,* suggests that first, you *observe* the problem or situation carefully. Notice the details. Next, *recognize* the absurdity or irony present. Ask yourself, who is here? What's going on? Are there power struggles? What are the emotions being experienced? Finally, *accept* the situation without attempting to control or change it.

I'm reminded of my friend, Frank. He was frequently ten to twenty minutes late for work each day. It was difficult for him to arrive at 9 AM because he was a single father with a disabled child. By the time he got his child to school and then drove across town to work, he was often a few minutes late. This didn't seem like a problem, because he worked extra during his lunch hour to make up the time. However, Frank's boss was very controlling and insisted that all employees arrive promptly. One day, the boss chastised Frank in front of his co-workers and announced that if he were ever late again, he would be fired. Frank was embarrassed. He vowed to get an earlier start the next day and prevent any tardiness. Unfortunately, despite of his sincere efforts, he was delayed by a traffic jam and walked into the office at 9:15 AM. His boss stood scowling in the middle of the office and his co-workers anxiously awaited the confrontation. Frank put down his briefcase, walked up to his boss, offered to shake hands and announced, "Hello sir, my name is Frank Jones. I'd like to apply for the position that became available about fifteen minutes ago." After a tense moment, the boss, trying hard to contain a smile, replied, "Get to work, Frank."

Of course, Frank could have handled the situation in any number of serious ways. But, because he was able to see, recognize and accept the situation, he could create a humorous response to the problem. Frank could *see* that he was caught, and that there was no way to sneak in unnoticed. He *recognized* that the boss was not about to lose face by accepting an excuse in front of his co-workers. And finally, Frank *accepted* that his job was gone, so he had nothing to lose by asking to be his own replacement!

Steps to Find and Create Humor

1) Exaggerate and overstate the problem.

> Making the situation bigger than life helps us to regain an humorous perspective. Cartoon caricatures, slapstick comedy, and clowning antics are all based on exaggeration.

> Brian Moench is a physician and cartoonist who has created *In Your Face Cards,* a collection of humorous calendars and note cards about health care. One of my favorites depicts an operating room where the surgeon is holding a tube. One end is stuck in a patient, who has only arms, legs and a head, but is missing her entire middle section. The other end of the tube leads into a bottle containing the patient's torso.

The caption reads, "During Mrs. Jones' suction lipectomy, there was a sudden power surge."

2) Look for the irony.

Irony is the difference between how things are and how they should be. Irony helps us identify the craziness that exists in our society. To spot the little 'ironies' ask yourself, "Why is it that.." or "Have you ever wondered why..."

Comedian Gallager, famous for his "Sledge-o-matic" routine where he smashes fresh, juicy fruit all over the audience, asks us to think about this irony, "Why is it that when you bounce a check at the bank, they charge you more of what they know you haven't got enough of in the first place?"

3) Recognize the incongruities and the nonsense of a difficult situation.

In her book, *And How Are We Feeling Today?*, Kathryn Hammer suggests some pretty nonsensical ways to prepare for hospitalization:

♥ Lay on the front lawn dressed in paper napkins with straws stuck up your nose and ask people to poke you as they go by.

♥ Put your hand down the garbage disposal while practicing your smile and repeating, 'Mild discomfort.'

♥ Remove all actual food from the house.

♥ Learn to urinate in an empty lipstick tube.

4) Learn to play with words.

Create puns and 'spoonerisms.' Don Hauptman suggests a few wacky ones in his book, *Cruel and Unusual Puns:*

♥ Sign on a diaper truck: "Rock a dry baby."

♥ Kazoo players' love song: "You'd be so Nice to Hum Comb To."

♥ Commercial for Crayola crayons: "It's enough to make your kin scrawl."

♥ Sign on a divorce lawyer's wall: "Satisfaction guaranteed, or your honey back."

5) Learn to appreciate SURPRISE!

The surprise ending of a joke stimulates laughter. It derails our "train of thought." If you are a person who likes to maintain control and predict every conceivable outcome, you probably don't like surprises. The funniness of a joke depends upon its "surprise" element. Learn to appreciate surprise and you will laugh a whole lot more!

*You've got to realize when all goes well,
and everything is beautiful, you have no comedy.
It's when somebody steps on the bride's train, or belches
during the ceremony that you've got comedy!*

—Phyllis Diller

How to Find Humor Anywhere, Anytime, Anyplace

Finding Tension Relief in Humor

If you can spontaneously create and share a comical perspective on an uncomfortable situation, you will be described as a humorous person! I remember Karen, a recently graduated nurse who was starting her first job on a Pediatric Unit. Other nurses had warned her about a particular physician who had a reputation for being extremely critical, impatient, and easily angered. They suggested that she try to prevent his angry outbursts by anticipating his needs and providing solutions before he could get upset. One morning during hospital rounds, he decided to check the level of a child's heart with the monitoring equipment next to the bed. When he demanded a yard stick, Karen told him they didn't have one on the unit. Gruffly he said, "Well, just get me any kind of straight stick." Karen hurried to the playroom and brought back a small child-sized broom, which met the physician's needs.

Early the next morning, the physician arrived on the Unit and walked toward the same child's room. Karen hurried up to him and asked, "Will you be needing your broom today, doctor?" He smiled at her and said, "No, dear. I drove my car." At first she was surprised, then seeing the twinkle in his eye, she broke into a broad smile, and then, both of them began to laugh. Their playful joking released some tension and, because the physician poked fun at himself, Karen felt more tolerant of his impatient demands.

Tell stories and share jokes created by someone else. Some people can remember an incredible number and variety of jokes. If you can't, write a funny joke down so you can re-tell it. Telling jokes helps people laugh, but it is not nearly as therapeutic as helping people laugh at their own unique situation. See the absurdity of your circumstances, and begin to relax!

As a full time speaker, I travel frequently on commercial airlines. During one winter, severe weather patterns caused delayed flights and missed connections. I was stranded at Chicago's O'Hare Airport. Many frustrated travelers complained to the gate attendants about the inconvenience. One particularly irate gentleman was vehemently complaining to the attendant about missing a very important meeting. Loudly, he demanded to speak to the person responsible for this situation. The attendant patiently listened to the passenger and then agreed, "You're right, you should speak directly to the one in charge. Let me get him on the phone for you." She picked up the phone, punched some numbers and said, "Hello, God. . . there's a gentleman here who wants an explanation for this unfortunate delay." Whether the traveler enjoyed this little joke as much as I did is difficult to say, but he did smile a wee bit.

On another flight, passengers were shocked into wakefulness by a rather abrupt and severe landing. As we anxiously looked at each other, the flight attendant calmly announced, "Well, ladies and gentlemen, if our coffee doesn't wake you up, our landings sure will!"

About twenty years ago, I was working in the Coronary Care Unit of a small hospital in California. Rest and relaxation was important for patients, so there were no phones in the rooms. If the patient received a call and was awake and stable, the nurses would bring a phone into the room and transfer the call to the patient. One particular patient had a sporadic problem with his cardiac rhythm. His heart would suddenly begin to beat rapidly in a pattern that we call ventricular tachycardia (dangerous and potentially life threatening). Often, a patient will be fully conscious but unaware of the problem, which is in itself dangerous, as it can progress to a lethal pattern called ventricular fibrillation or cardiac arrest. At this time, the recommended initial treatment was to give a "precordial thump" where you hit the patient's chest quite firmly with your fist!

We had just brought the phone into Joe's room so that he could talk with his wife, when his heart rhythm changed into ventricular tachycardia. The intern saw this on the cardiac monitor in the nursing station and ran into the room. Without any explanation, he punched Joe firmly on the chest. The action was successful and a normal heart pattern was restored, but I'll never forget the surprised look on Joe's face as he looked up at the intern and said, "Gee if you wanted to use the phone, all you had to do was ask!"

Tip: To Evaluate Your Sense Of Humor, Ask Yourself,

- ♥ Do I see the existence or possibility of amusing stories in the absurd moments in my life?

- ♥ Do I spontaneously laugh out loud when I notice something funny?

- ♥ Am I able to share my amusing insights with others?

Finding Humor In Difficult Situations

The word "humor" is derived from its Latin root, "umor" which means to be fluid and flow like water. Our ability to recognize humor increases as we become more flexible in our perceptions, thoughts, and attitudes. A sense of humor helps us to see new possibilities in difficult situations, feel larger than the problem, and change the perceptions of our circumstances before the circumstances change us. We are empowered.

Janet Henry, a fun loving wife and mother of four, was diagnosed with breast cancer in her forties. She was frightened: afraid of dying, afraid of leaving her children, and her husband. Her physician recommended a radical mastectomy followed by chemotherapy. Suddenly, the body she had lived with for forty-five years changed. Her chest had a hideous scar where her breast had been, the chemotherapy caused her hair to fall out and she began to lose weight because of the persistent nausea. In spite of this suffering and loss, Janet maintained her sense of humor and used it to help her cope with the uncomfortable changes. Before her illness, Janet had written funny poems to describe amusing aspects of motherhood and family life. After surgery, she continued to write humorous poems about her new life and routines.

These poems, collected in a booklet entitled, *Surviving the Cure*, reveal Janet's courage and ability to see the blessings of her life despite her unfortunate diagnosis. Her humorous perspective strengthens and inspires others who are in a similar predicament:

The Nightly Ritual
I prop my wig on the dresser,
And tuck my prosthesis beneath,
And thank God, I still go to bed with
My man and my very own teeth!

Humor helps us cope with the unknown and communicate more effectively. Nurses often give patients information to help them understand and prepare for procedures. When patients know what to expect, they feel more relaxed and cooperative. We may need to talk about subjects that are usually personal and private. To help ease the patient's embarrassment we may describe things in an amusing way. Leslie Gibson, a nurse at Morton Plant Hospital in Clearwater, Florida tells about how she helped one man prepare for surgery. Leslie had explained that his food and fluids would be limited after surgery due to the sluggish activity of the bowels. She also explained that the hospital staff would ask if he had passed gas. Once he began passing gas, he would be ready to eat and drink again. She then pulled out a whoopee cushion and squeezed the air out of it's tight sphincter, creating that sound we usually find embarrassing. She reassured the patient that, for nurses, that sound was music to their ears. The patient howled with relief at the light-hearted permission to heal naturally.

Finding Humor in Tragedy

Humor enhances our ability to recognize the comical aspects of tragic situations. Captain Gerald Coffee was a prisoner of war in Vietnam for several years. He describes the horrible, inhumane conditions in the POW camps in his book, *Beyond Survival.* The Viet Cong isolated American soldiers, hoping the loneliness would break their spirits. They were not allowed to see or talk with each other. Yet, even with the threat of punishment, the GI's would use morse code to tap out messages and jokes to each other. Coffee describes the dismal meals they were given, sometimes plain bread and water. Even then, the bread was old and moldy. One morning, as he bit into his bread he saw a weevil, so he spontaneously composed a poem, "Oh little weevil in my bread . . . I have just bit off your head!"

Throughout his book, Coffee describes how the prisoners used humor to tolerate the degrading conditions and to keep their spirits strong. Once a month, the soldiers were allowed to shower. During one shower, Captain

Coffee noticed a message scratched on the wall. He leaned down to read it, and burst into laughter. The message said: "Smile! You're on Candid Camera!" This moment of absurdity amidst the horrors of war provided a few moments of laughter that was so essential for survival. Coffee explains, "Laughter sets the spirit free to move through even the most tragic circumstances. It helps us shake our heads clear, get our feet back under us, and restore our sense of balance and purpose. Humor is essential to our peace of mind and our ability to go beyond survival" (pp. 131-132).

Finding Humor In The Face Of Death

I have personally witnessed this "laughing spirit" while attending the death of a hospice patient in San Francisco. His family called me at 2:00 AM and I rushed to his house, braced for another night of lost sleep while supporting a grieving family. When I arrived, Charley was near death. He was exhibiting the breathing pattern of impending death: frequent periods of apnea (breathlessness), lasting up to a minute. His family was solemnly gathered in the room. At one point his breathing paused for a particularly long moment. His wife stood up and remarked, "Well, the waiting is over. Charley has passed away." Then, to our surprise, Charley began to breathe again!

After a few moments of hand-wringing anticipation, Charley's breathing stopped once more. This time the pause was even longer. His grown son stood up like a giant in the room and announced, "It's over, Dad's finally gone." Suddenly Charley snored loudly and began to breath again. Exasperated, Charley's wife slapped her hand on the bedside table and exclaimed, "Well, isn't that just like Charley to keep us all waiting!" Everyone burst into laughter. I'm sure Charley was laughing too!

Finding Humor in a Disaster

Humor can be a psychological strategy that gives us relief from pain, suffering, or tragedy. This "survivor" humor is used by people who have experienced misfortune, or by society as a whole when confronted with a shocking tragedy or large scale disaster (e.g., earthquakes, hurricanes, tragic accidents).

During the mid-west flooding in 1993, one bill-board cleverly announced, "Questions about the weather? Call 1-800-NOAH." Another sign in Missouri, the "Show Me" state, proclaimed, "Welcome to Missouri, Now the Row Me State." Or, how about this one, "The weather lately gives a whole new meaning to Roe vs. Wade." After the Los Angeles earthquake in 1989, a sign on the front lawn of a demolished house announced, "House for rent—some assembly required." After the Rodney King beating, some people in Los Angeles sported T-Shirts with the saying, "LAPD—We'll treat you like a King." These epithets reflect our sense of humor in the face of disastrous, overwhelming situations. They unite us and remind us that we are not alone in our suffering.

Sandy Ritz, R.N. M.S., is completing her doctoral thesis at the University of Hawaii School of Public Health. Sandy's research explores the use of humor during disasters. She has studied the kinds of humor used during the different stages of disaster recovery and the different types of humor preferred by disaster victims and rescue workers. Sandy's research focused primarily on the victims and workers of Hurricane Iniki in 1992 on the island of Kauai. She also examined earthquakes in San Francisco and Los Angeles, firestorms in Santa Barbara and Oakland, California and victims of Hurricane Hugo in Miami. Though her final research data is still being analyzed, Sandy has already confirmed several important facts: humor is almost always used to cope with the shock and discomfort of any disaster; different types of humor are used and appreciated by victims and by disaster workers; and, the styles of preferred humor change as people move through the different phases of recovery after a disaster (Ritz, 1995).

Mental health specialists at the National Institute for Mental Health, have identified emotional phases that survivors experience following a disaster (Farberow & Frederick, 1978). Sandy's work identifies the different types of humor that are used or avoided in each of these phases. An understanding of these recovery phases assists both victims and disaster workers in using humor as a coping strategy.

Disaster Recovery Phases

The Heroic Phase. This phase occurs at the time of impact and immediately afterward when energy is expended helping others survive. If there is any humor, it is spontaneous and is used to relieve tension and overcome fear. Two hikers were caught on a precarious coastal trail when Hurricane Iniki struck the Island of Kauai. The winds were so fierce they were almost blown off the trail into the sea below. Hanging on for dear life, the hikers maintained their courage and relieved their anxiety by singing the theme song from the television show, "Gilligan's Island!" This type of humor helped them find some relief from the incredible strain they were under.

The Honeymoon Phase. This period may last from one week to six months and embraces 'recovery optimism.' Survivors experience great joy in just being alive and feel the support and caring of relief efforts. Their losses, difficulties ahead, and negative emotions are denied. The humor used in this phase is positive, upbeat, and it laughs at the absurdity of the situation without alot of anger. After the hurricane hit Kauai, people wore T-shirts emblazoned with, "Landscaped by Iniki" or "House for sale—best deal of the century!"

The Disillusionment Phase. This stage can last from two months to two years. This is a time of grieving, with feelings of disappointment, anger and resentment. Relief programs are withdrawn and victims concentrate on rebuilding their own lives. Survivors may feel isolated, angry and pessimistic, and can easily take offense at attempts of humor. Aggressive humor (satire, ridicule, and irony) is used by disaster victims to express their sense of powerlessness. The target of their humor is often disaster workers and others in power. After Hurricane Andrew hit Florida, one T- shirt proclaimed, "I survived Hurricane Andrew, but FEMA (Federal Emergency Maintenance Association) is killing me." Joking from anyone perceived as an outsider, even disaster workers, is not appreciated by survivors during this phase and can be easily misinterpreted.

The Reconstruction Phase. This final phase may last for several years, and is a time of rebuilding and recovery. Humor returns slowly and reflects a sense of community. It acknowledges the community's collective fears, goals, problems, and includes acceptance and adaptation to change. Survivors share a common bond and along with that, a 'shared humor' about their circumstances. After two years of disasters in the Los Angeles area, residents began to assert, "Los Angeles has four distinct seasons: Earthquake, Flood, Firestorm and Mud Slide!"

The Different Uses of Humor

Hoping Humor

The ability to hope for something better enables human beings to cope with difficult situations such as disasters, depravation, failure, loneliness, and suffering. During the Holocaust, many called humor the "currency of hope." Prisoners in the concentration camps used humor as both a psychological tool and a defense mechanism. Humor was a bond among trusted friends, a protective shield, and a morale booster (Lipman, 1991).

Psychiatrist Viktor Frankl was a survivor of the concentration camp at Auschwitz. He observed that humor was an essential factor in the prognosis for survival. He would encourage others in the camp to invent at least one amusing story each day about an incident that could happen some time after their liberation. A surgeon friend had been an assistant on the staff of a large hospital. "I once tried to get him to smile by describing to him how he would be unable to lose the habits of camp life when he returned to his former work. At the camp, the German foremen would encourage us to work faster by shouting: 'Action! Action!' I told my friend, 'One day you will be back in the operating room, performing a big abdominal operation. Suddenly an orderly will rush in announcing the arrival of the senior surgeon by shouting, 'Action! Action!'" Frankl's optimistic spirit predicted an end to the war, the defeat of the Germans and the triumphant return of the victims to better lives. He gave the prisoners hope and the strength to withstand the suffering.

Frankl, in his book, *Man's Search for Meaning*, writes about the importance of humor in coping with the degrading and frightening conditions of the camps. The capacity to laugh at oneself and one's predicament provided detachment from the horror, yet also forced one to recognize it. "While we were waiting for the shower, our nakedness was brought home to us; we really had nothing now except our bare bodies—even minus hair, all we possessed, literally, was our naked existence . . . Thus the illusions some of us still held were destroyed one by one, and then, quite unexpectedly, most of us were overcome by a grim sense of humor. We knew that we had nothing to lose except our so ridiculously naked lives. When the showers started to run, we all tried very hard to make fun, both about ourselves and about each other. After all, real water did flow from the sprays!" (p. 24).

I never would have made it if I could not have laughed.
It lifted me momentarily out of this horrible situation,
just enough to make it livable.

—Viktor Frankl

Coping Humor

Disasters, traumas, and illness create stress not only for the victims and patients, but also for their family and caregivers. Stress disrupts our ability to function smoothly. Coping is the word we use to describe what we do to minimize this disruption. In any illness, patients must cope with the fear of pain and suffering, lack of privacy, loss of choice and control over very simple parts of their lives. Families must cope with the burden of finding enough time and energy to provide care for their loved one, struggling with a combative patient or protecting a confused one. Professional caregivers must cope with the demands of providing more complex care with less staff, deal with administrative paperwork and, handle the emotional exhaustion of witnessing suffering and death on a daily basis. How effectively we cope with these challenges will determine our success in providing care or in recovering from illness. To cope effectively, we must change how we think and how we behave in situations of stress (Benner & Wrubel, 1989).

Nurses, physicians, and other health care professionals cope daily with the reality and horror of illness, suffering, and death. Our compassion and caring may leave us vulnerable to feelings of sympathy for those we serve. There is a great difference between sympathy and empathy. Both arise from compassion and caring, but they relate to the suffering person in different ways. Sympathy feels the "other's pain" as if it were our own; we feel frightened with them, angry with them, depressed with them. As you might imagine, sympathy decreases our effectiveness as caregivers because we lose our objective perspective. Empathy, on the other hand, employs a "detached concern." We still express our compassion and caring, but without identifying with the patient's pain as if it were our own (Gaut & Leininger, 1991).

Humor is a coping tool that provides us with a similar "detached" perspective to empathy. Caregivers will often use humor as a means of maintaining some distance from the suffering and protecting themselves from a sympathetic response. Christina Maslach, in her book, *Burnout: The Cost of Caring,* describes how nurses use humor and laughter to cope with the stress and horror they frequently witness. "Sometimes things are so frustrating that to keep from crying, you laugh at a situation that may not be funny. You laugh, but in your heart you know what's really happening. Nevertheless, you do it because your own needs are important—we're all human beings and we have to be ourselves" (p. 102).

Our ability to laugh provides us with a momentary release from the intensity of what otherwise might be overwhelming. We use humor to gain a new perspective and to find a way to function in a situation that could otherwise be intolerable (Wooten, 1996).

Coping With Illness

Humor provides a voice for our pain and hopelessness. It offers a cathartic release, and then fills us with optimism and hope by helping us to laugh in the middle of our suffering.

> *"To truly laugh, you must be able to take your pain and play with it!"*
>
> *—Charlie Chaplin*

Humor requires a playful frame of mind that helps us detach from our problems and not take a serious situation so personally. When we observe others laughing at their difficult situation, it offers us hope and shows us that we can laugh at ourselves, too! Robert Lipsyte was diagnosed with cancer. As he struggled to recover from the surgery and chemotherapy, Robert used humor to create a positive attitude. Not everyone finds what they need from warm and gentle humor. Some people need a type of humor that is perhaps more rugged and realistic. Robert was one of these people. He enjoyed humor that could express his frustrations and anger. He believed that this "tumor humor" was an essential part of his recovery, because it kept him flexible. He wrote:

> "Attitude is everything in recovery from cancer. You gotta have 'tude if you expect to take a licking and come back ticking. Tumor humor is not warm and friendly, it's scrappy and sometimes nasty and tasteless, a sort of chemotherapy for the spirit—necessary but not always nice. The most important part of a fighting attitude is humor, because it keeps you loose."

Robert Lipsyte - Cancer survivor

Other cancer survivors are spreading the word about the therapeutic effects of humor. Jane Hill of Santa Ana, California was diagnosed with breast cancer in 1991. At that time, she was self-employed as a management consultant, and her daughter Kelly was only ten years old. Jane received her diagnosis only six months after she'd completed a course in stand-up comedy at her local community college. Fortunately for her, those skills were fresh in her mind and she began to view her treatment and recovery experience through the eyes of a comedian. After her diagnosis, she struggled through four surgeries within six months, during which time her breast was removed. Although none of that is funny, Jane believes that it was her humor skills that gave her the distance she needed to laugh about some of the most embarrassing moments.

Jane created a comedy routine that includes some of those moments, like the time she went swimming and noticed that her breast prosthesis had slipped out of her bathing suit and was floating about the pool in full view of everybody! Embarrassing at the time, but wonderful material for comedy later. Jane is a joyful survivor and an inspiration for others to *Keep Laughing to Keep Healthy,* the title of her forthcoming book. Jane travels throughout the U.S. speaking and performing for cancer support groups and at national cancer survivor conventions (See Appendix).

Comedy is the main weapon we have against 'The Horror.' With it we can strike a blow at death itself. Or, at least, poke a hole in the pretentious notion that there is something dignified about it.

—John Callahan

The talented comedian Gilda Radner portrayed the zany character, Roseanna Roseannadana on the TV comedy show, Saturday Night Live. At the peak of her performing career and soon after she married fellow comedian and love of her life, Gene Wilder, Gilda began having unusual stomach pains. Her physician discovered advanced stages of ovarian cancer. During her three year battle with cancer, she kept a journal of her experiences and captured them with the same pungent wit and irreverence we saw in her comedy routines. Joanna Bull, her counselor during this time, describes Gilda as "the archetypal clown, always able to find the funny side of any situation" (Wooten, 1995c).

Gilda was a member of the Wellness Community in Santa Monica, California, a patient support group. The center provides an opportunity for patients and their families to share their experience and to help others find ways to cope with the challenges of life threatening illness. Each week, they have a "Jokefest" and group members bring a joke to share. Awards are given for the best jokes, especially jokes about cancer. One week the best joke was,

> Q: What do you call a person with
>   recurrent lymphoma?
> A: A lymphomaniac!

Gilda was an inspiration for her group with her courage and humor. She helped them to see the potential for comedy in their battle with cancer. Gilda left a legacy for us all in her book, *It's Always Something,* which chronicles her struggles, her hopes, her frustrations and most of all her ability to find the humorous parts of her illness.

Joanna and Gene have recently completed a project that fulfills one of Gilda's last wishes. Gilda's Club, headquartered in New York City with local chapters throughout the U.S., offers a center for education, networking and support for patients and families facing the diagnosis and treatment of cancer. Through lectures, discussion groups and social activities, they seek to provide members with comfort, support, and skills to live with cancer. Humor skills, ala Gilda, are taught to help patients and families cope with illness.

Cancer is probably the most unfunny thing in the world, but I'm a comedian, and even cancer couldn't stop me from seeing the humor in what I went through.

—Gilda Radner

Robert, Jane and Gilda found courage and hope in humor. They laughed when they could and cried when they needed to. They send a message for us to do the same. We have the power to choose how we look at our circumstances. Don't deny the reality of your situation, but rather, be open to the possibility that amusing events can occur in even the most challenging circumstances.

There are two appropriate responses to frustration, you can laugh or you can cry. I prefer laughter, because there's less mopping up to do afterwards!

—Kurt Vonnegut

Patient Support Groups

Like Gilda's Club, support groups provide a place for patients facing an illness and undergoing treatments to talk about their struggles, doubts and success. Each member has a credibility that goes beyond the textbook understanding of professionals. The group members have lived through a common trauma and have learned to cope with the lifestyle changes created by their illness. Members who can find the humor in their own experience can help others find the humor in their situation.

Support groups form around different illnesses. Mastectomy patients attend "Reach for Recovery," those who have had their larynx (voice box) removed may join the "Lost Chord" group. The support group for heart surgery patients is called "Mended Hearts," a national organization with local chapters. One of the members of the Orange County, California "Mended Hearts" chapter was Stewart Duncan. He wrote humorous poems about his life and how his illness had changed it. Duncan's book, *Please Don't Step on my Catheter* was published by the Orange County Chapter of the American Heart Association. His book provides many amusing examples of the humorous side of this life threatening situation. I can almost hear him chuckle as he poured his frustrations into verse. Duncan found hope in his laughter when his heart was breaking:

The Mended Hearts

We who've joined the Mended Hearts,
can shyly boast of the mended parts.
There's courage and daring to rate,
when heart trained surgeons operate.
And of all the patients, we're the stars
when it comes to boasting scars.
But here's what seems like heck to me,
the lowly hemmroidectomy.
Painful, itchy, done up-ended.
Can they boast of what's been mended?
And what a lousy deal they got,
joining mended "you know what."

Gallows Humor

"Gallows humor" is a type of medical humor usually seen as hostile, inappropriate, or "just plain sick," by the people who are unfamiliar with healthcare professions. Gallows humor acknowledges the disgusting or intolerable aspects of a situation, and attempts to transform it into something lighthearted and amusing (Rosenberg, 1991).

When I was working in the Emergency Room at a county hospital, an ambulance brought in a homeless person they had found unconscious in an alley. The man was filthy, his breath reeked of alcohol, and he had lice crawling on his body. It took two of us more than an hour just to clean him up enough for admission. It was difficult work and our senses were overwhelmed with unpleasant sights and smells. I read the intern's admission note on the way up in the elevator. It said, "Patient carried into E.R. by Army of body lice, who were chanting, "Save our host. Save our host." I laughed heartily at this amusing picture and suddenly my struggles of the last hours were put into a humorous perspective and I felt a lot less angry and a lot more compassion.

Samuel Shem, M.D., wrote a hilarious and often heart-rending book called, House of God. In it he described many shocking encounters during his medical internship. He introduced the term "G.O.M.E.R." His 'GOMER Assessment Scale' has been laughed at for years and added to by health professionals from all specialties. Shem defined G.O.M.E.R. to mean, "Get Out of My Emergency Room!" The patients who were given this nickname were usually very ill, often confused, uncooperative, and unappreciative of the help given by the hospital staff. Here's Dr. Shem's, GOMER Assessment Scale:

You have a GOMER on your hands if:

Their old chart weighs more than 5 pounds.

Their previous address was the VA Hospital.

They have a seizure and never drop their cigarette.

They tie their pajama strings into their foley catheter.

Their BUN is higher than their IQ.

It is important to note that gallows humor, so therapeutic for staff, may not be appreciated by patients or their families. Nurse anesthetist, Wayne Johnston, R.N., told of a time when a patient's family witnessed his laughter as he was washing up after an unsuccessful attempt at resuscitation:

> You saw me laugh after your father died... to you I must have appeared callused and uncaring... Please understand, much of the stress health care workers suffer comes about because we do care... Sooner or later, we will all laugh at the wrong time. I hope your father would under-stand that my laugh meant no disrespect; it was a grab at balance. I knew there was another patient who needed my full care and atten-tion... my laugh was no less cleansing for me than your tears were for you.
>
> —Wayne Johnston, RN

Humor is a coping tool for the health care professional. Lisa Rosenberg, R.N., Ph.D., is on the faculty of the Rush-Presbyterian-St. Luke's School of Nursing in Chicago. She studied the use of humor among staff in emergency rooms and critical care units. In a chapter in *Nursing Perspectives on Humor* she states, "Emergency personnel experience a wide spectrum of serious events—trauma, life-threatening illness, chaotic emotional situations—often all at the same time. There is no time to emotionally prepare for these events, and little time to ventilate or 'decompress.' The spontaneous way in which humor can be produced in almost any situation, and it's instantaneous stress-reducing effects are well suited to the emergency care experience." (p. 47).

During one of my humor workshops, a nurse manager gave me a sign that had been placed by the staff in the waiting room for visitors and family members to read. The staff hoped to educate and reassure the visitors that their use of humor as a coping tool helped them provide better care for their loved ones. The sign read:

> You may occasionally see us laughing,
> or even take note of some jest.
> Know that we are giving your loved one
> our care at it's very best.
> There are times when the tension is highest.
> There are times when our systems are stressed.
> We've discovered humor a factor
> in keeping our sanity blessed.
> So, if you're a patient in waiting,
> or a relative, or a friend of one seeing,
> don't hold our smiling against us,
> it's the way we keep from screaming.

Compassionate vs. Caustic Humor

Not all humor, whether hoping, coping or gallows, leaves us feeling light-hearted and relieved. Some types of humor are caustic and cause feelings of embarrassment, indignation, or threat. Compassionate humor—humor from the heart—leaves us feeling relaxed, accepted, and safe. Compassionate humor is helpful and healing. It connects people together. Caustic humor is hateful and harmful. It separates people with isolation and offense. When caustic humor is used, examine the heart space of the person creating this humor to understand their motive and intent. Following is a list of the characteristics of these types of humor:

Compassionate Humor	**Caustic Humor**
Creates bonds	Creates barriers
Reduces tension	Increases hostility and stress
Includes all people	Perpetuates elite stereo-types
Reduces discomfort	Increases defensiveness
Provides hope	Focuses on the negative
Moves us towards health	Moves us towards disease

The range of humor styles is broad. Most examples fall somewhere between compassionate and caustic. It is possible to see the same piece of humor from different perspectives, depending on the group you identify with. For example, nurses make jokes about doctors that doctors may consider caustic, yet it reduces tension and creates bonds among the nursing group. One such joke is:

Q: What do you call two orthopedic
     surgeons reading an EKG?
A: A double-blind study.

Similarly, physicians may create humor about malpractice attorneys to relieve tension and create inner group bonding against a common enemy. Like this common joke:

Q: If you find a lawyer buried up to his
     neck in cement, what does that mean?
A: Somebody ran out of cement.

Patients joke about the health care power structure to relieve their anger and frustrations. Many get-well cards poke fun at the medical team or hospital routines. Like the eight-five year-old man who complains to his physician about the pain in his left shoulder. The physician reassures him by saying, "Well, George, its eighty-five years old!" The patient responds by commenting, "Yeah, but my right shoulder is eighty-five years old too, and it doesn't hurt."

Some humor targets a common enemy of all three groups. Insurance companies frustrate both patients and health care providers by imposing rigid limitations on the care we wish to receive or provide. Jokes about insurance groups include this one, "The president of a successful HMO died and met with St. Peter at the Pearly Gates. The corporate executive expressed surprise that he actually qualified for Heaven after all the care he denied people just to save the company money. St. Peter reassured him that indeed, he did qualify, but his stay was only approved for three days." Whether one sees humor as caustic or compassionate will depend on who's the "butt" of the joke and whether we have feelings of animosity or resentment for them.

Offensive Humor

Taking offense to humor has two dynamics: those who give offense and those who take offense. Either one may destroy the enjoyment of shared humor. Those who 'give offense' are easy to spot. Usually, we label these people "jerks" and try to avoid their company. The other dynamic is more difficult to resolve. Some people seem to go out of their way to 'take offense,' and always seem to be within earshot of the joke you are sharing. Christian Hageseth in his book, *A Laughing Place,* suggests we are more cautious and hesitant to share amusement around people who are easily offended. Both the 'taker' and 'giver' of offense put a damper on sharing and showering in the spirit of fun.

Think about yourself. We have probably all been a 'giver' or a 'taker' at one time or another. Think about your reactions to different types of humor, what offends you and what delights you? What kinds of jokes do you tell? Pay attention to the humor you hear and see around you. Think about the times humor has offended or hurt you and the times when it has made your heart sing. Be conscious of humor and practice the type of humor that makes you feel good. Then we all share in the spirit of fun!!

Body - Mind - Spirit Connection

As it is not proper to cure the eyes without the head, nor the head without the body, so neither is it proper to cure the body without the soul.

—Socrates

We are much more than our physical bodies moving around this planet. We are also thinking, feeling, spiritual beings. What we think and feel influences how we use our physical body. For example, if we think people don't like us, we may sit with slumped posture, avoid eye contact, or hesitate before speaking. If we feel nervous, we might drum our fingers on the table, tap our foot or stutter. The mind affects the body and soul. Our spiritual awareness encourages us to open our hearts to compassion, and to let go of our busyness and striving. We become still and listen. It is in that stillness that we feel a connection with all things and a oneness with the universe. We experience true freedom, for we are fully open, honest, and loving toward the next person, the next moment, and the fullness of life as it is. Our bodies are relaxed and our minds are at peace.

Illness can damage the body, overwhelm the mind, and break the spirit. Disease causes an imbalance in the energy flowing between the body, mind and spirit. When we become ill, we desire to be healed. It is interesting to note that the verb, "to heal" comes from the Latin word, "Haelen," which means to 'make whole.' To become whole again means to balance our physical body, our mental thoughts and our spiritual awareness.

When we allow ourselves to laugh on a daily basis as well as during difficult or stressful times, we can facilitate our own healing. Humor can help make us whole again, by triggering laughter which strengthens the body; by engaging the mind to perceive new possibilities; and, by opening the spirit to feel connected with the universe. Humor can stimulate healing in our physical body, bring peace to our emotions, and strengthen our will to live.

Body

Mirthful laughter (laughter at what we consider to be truly funny) has been proven to have a profound effect on the body, mind, and spirit. Laughter is a wonderful tonic for the body: our heart beats stronger, our blood flows more briskly, and more oxygen is delivered to our cells. We breathe deeper and exhale more fully, clearing our lungs of stale air. Many muscles are activated as we laugh: the diaphragm, the intercostal muscles, the abdominal muscles (Fry, 1971; Fry, 1986). Research has proven that mirthful laughter can stimulate our immune system, increase our protection against viruses, bacteria and, even cancer (Berk & Tan, 1991).

When we are ill, the body naturally slows down. Sometimes this inactivity is due to fatigue, sometimes to pain, and sometimes to depression. When we are immobile, the body suffers. Blood no longer moves briskly through our vessels. Our breathing becomes shallow. Our muscles weaken. A vicious cycle begins, spiraling us into more serious problems. Illness may require us to quit work, be hospitalized, or give up our family and leisure activities. These losses may lead to depression, which further weakens the immune system, and leaves us more vulnerable to attack by virus and bacteria. This is when the benefits of mirthful laughter help to offset the changes that occur from illness and immobilization. "Laugh yourself healthy!" may be your healing motto. The physiological research on laughter is discussed more thoroughly in Chapter 3, The Healing Heart.

Mind

Humor is a cognitive skill that uses both sides of the brain. The left side of the cerebral cortex is active during the telling of a joke, but as the humor is perceived, (as we "get it") the brain wave activity moves toward the right side of the cerebral cortex. Humor brings together the whole brain, linking the logical left brain with the creative right brain. Several research studies have shown that after perceiving something humorous, we become more creative at problem solving (Dunn, 1995).

Dr. Alice Isen of the Department of Psychology at Cornell University, believes that laughter increases creativity and flexibility of thought. Her research has shown that people who had just viewed a short comedy film were better able to devise innovative approaches to problems than those who had not seen the film. She believed that the comedic view inspired movement from "functional fixedness" to "creative flexibility" (Isen, 1987). Other research demonstrates that creative people are more drawn to humor (McGhee, 1979). Avner Ziv of the University of Tel Aviv, has shown that exposing high school students to a semester-long humor training program increased their creativity (Ziv, 1989). So humor can do more for us than tickle our funny bone, it might just help us discover it, or paint it, or at least laugh at it!

Several years ago, I worked in a Neurological Intensive Care Unit caring for people recovering from brain surgery or head injuries. It is important to recognize changes in the cognitive abilities of these patients because if the brain begins to swell one of the first symptoms will be a change in orientation and sensorium. Patients are asked to provide answers to basic questions every hour to assess for changes. The questions include, "What year is it? Where are you? Who is the president?" The Unit I worked on had floor to ceiling windows looking out from the seventh floor. My patient had a bed next to the window, and as I asked him a few questions, he answered slowly, with his eyes closed. I was concerned. But, his answer to my next question reassured me that I need not worry. I said, "Mr. Green, do you know where you are?" He opened his swollen eyes and peered slowly around the room and out the window, and then answered, "Well, I'm either in heaven or the ICU." Why do you say that?" I asked. "Because I'm awfully high up and I get everything I want." In that moment I knew his brain was functioning normally, because he was clever enough to make a simple joke.

Spirit

Spirit and spirituality are different from religion and religiosity. Religion is an institution with rituals and beliefs intended to help people on their spiritual journey. It is possible to be deeply involved in religion and never have a spiritual experience. Spirituality is a personal and highly individual experience. It is our spirit that connects us with other humans, animals and the whole of life itself. Spiritual understanding offers answers to how we fit into the scheme of life and death. Humor expressed with compassion, also connects us with others and is evidence of a strong spirit. Great spiritual leaders have a quick sense of humor and a free and easy laugh. When Ghandi was asked by a reporter, "Mahatma Gi, what do you think of western civilization?" Ghandi replied, "I think it would be a good idea."

When we use humor with warmth and sensitivity, it expresses our compassion and caring. I remember a young male patient that I was caring for who was bleeding profusely from the vessels lining his stomach and esophagus. In addition to pumping blood into him, we'd inserted a special tube into his esophagus with a balloon on the end. We then inflated the balloon to secure the position in his esophagus and applied traction by pulling on the tube, then tied it to the face shield of a football helmet which the patient wore. The bleeding was uncontrolled for several days as the patient's condition worsened.

The nurses cared deeply for this young man. We were all sad about his imminent death. Perhaps he noticed our sadness, because one morning he called us over to the bedside, pointed at his helmet and asked, "What team am I on?" We all laughed and cried at the same time. Humor has the power to connect us together and allows our spirits to unite in compassion.

The human race has only one really effective weapon,
and that's laughter. The moment it arises,
all our hardnesses yield, all our irritations and resentments
slip away, and a sunny spirit takes their place.

—Mark Twain

Burnout and Hardiness Factors

Professional caregivers, whether they are doctors, nurses, social workers, therapists, or counselors, are at risk for burn-out. One of the most common symptoms of burn-out is a sense of powerlessness. If the problems we must attend to are too complex or numerous, we feel overwhelmed. We begin to feel frustrated, angry, and hopeless. To protect ourselves, we may withdraw, withhold our caring efforts, or even quit the profession. Yet, some people seem to have a resilient nature and experience much less burnout.

Sociologist Suzanne Kobasa, has described this type of person as possessing "hardiness factors." After years of studying professionals with stressful jobs, she has identified three personality factors that help us to cope with stress, maintain our health and prevent burnout (Kobasa, 1983). These hardiness factors are Commitment, Challenge, and Control.

If we are to survive in a stressful profession, we must establish a *commitment* to ourselves, our profession, and the people we serve. We must develop an ability to see potential change as a *challenge* rather than a threat. We must accept that the *location of control* for our own life lies within us and not outside of us. I believe that our ability to maintain a humorous perspective will strengthen each of these hardiness factors.

Tools To Develop Hardiness

Commitment. Get involved in the decision making processes on your unit or in your facility. Speak to The Lions Club, Rotary, Jr. League, and Church groups about health and wellness. Develop a self care program that includes exercise, meditation, recreation, and humor.

Challenge. Continue to grow and develop professionally with continuing education programs. Network with other nurses and brainstorm solutions for problems you share. Remind yourself, the only time things stop changing is when you're dead!

Control. Learn assertiveness and communication skills. Remember that surrender and letting go is a choice you can make. Remind yourself of your successes.

Humor can strengthen our commitment to our profession and the people we serve. It helps us maintain optimism, and keeps our hearts open to our patients and colleagues. Sharing moments of playfulness and laughter on the job will strengthen the connection we feel with our colleagues and provide an opportunity to "let off a little steam." This cathartic release clears our heads, energizes our bodies and renews our spirits.

Humor prepares us for the challenge of change by stimulating our creativity and expanding our vision. With this expanded perspective we can see a greater number of possible solutions to the problems we face. This perceptual flexibility helps us to cope with the many unknown aspects of change. Armed with a sense of humor, we are better prepared to meet the challenge of change rather than succumbing to its threat.

Our sense of control increases when we apply our humor skills during stressful times. Humor allows us to detach from the problem, to see our situation from a whole new point of view, and perhaps, notice some absurd and ridiculous aspects. Then it allows us to stand back and laugh!

Helpful Hints to Find & Maintain Your Sense of Humor

How can we as health care professionals keep our hearts open and continue to provide compassionate care? How can we smile and maintain our enthusiasm when healthcare reform forces us to "do more with less?" How can we maintain our commitment, face the challenges and stay in control? Humor provides an answer. By finding a humorous perspective and allowing ourselves to laugh about the frustrations and heartbreaking situations we face each day, we acquire the strength and courage to keep on going. But how can we find anything to laugh about when patients are suffering, families are grieving, physicians are demanding and administrators are unavailable to hear our concerns about protecting the quality of care?

A Humor Journal for Nurses

Doug Fletcher, a Critical Care nurse from Mesa, Arizona has created a journal to provide nurses with the opportunity to laugh about their struggles and frustrations. Now entering its sixth year of publication, the *Journal of Nursing Jocularity* has over 35,000 subscribers from each of the 50 states and across Canada. This quarterly journal is a collection of true stories, cartoons, parodies, book reviews, interviews and much, much more. It has the quality and substance to qualify for inclusion in the Cumulative Index to Nursing and Allied Health Literature. I am honored to be a contributing editor and featured columnist (See Humor Resource List).

One issue published just before Christmas had a special section entitled, "Nursing Notes." Here is a song that one nurse wrote to provide a bit of seasonal humor and whimsy. Enjoy!

Jingle Bells
Susan Elaine Arnold, R.N., B.S.N., C.C.R.N.

Dashing down the hall, a stretcher in my way,
I just heard someone call, for a nurse in room 4-A.
The lab is on the phone, the charts are stacked galore,
I go into my patient's room and he is on the floor.
Ooooh!

Jingle bells, jingle bells, much to my dismay,
I am stuck at work again, twelve hours on Christmas Day!
Jingle bells, jingle bells, Christmas go away,
This is not my idea of a happy holiday.

A day or two ago, I thought I'd call in sick,
Just spend my Christmas Day at home,
Now wouldn't that be slick?
But as the time grew near, the guilt set in so fast,
I came to work and should have known that
Nice guys finish last.
Oooh!

Jingle bells, Jingle bells, O' my aching back,
This could drive me crazy, give me a heart attack!
Jingle bells, jingle bells, I don't hear them ring,
Christmas is no fun this year, I wish that it were spring.

Another patient said, as I answered her light,
"Would you please check my bed? It doesn't seem just right."
I take a closer look, I don't like this one bit,
She's had a dose of Milk of Mag, her bed is full of !#?@
Oooh!

Jingle bells, jingle bells, I don't mean to bitch,
I would not be here today if I had married rich.
Jingle bells, jingle bells, blast the mistletoe!
This will be the death of me, an awful way to go.

"Oh, honey you're so sweet, to take such care of me,
These nurses can't be beat, you're all so good, you see."
If what she says is true, before my song is sung.
One consolation that I have—the good, they say, die young!
Oooh!

Jingle bells, jingle bells—Santa, I'm so sad,
Guess I must have misbehaved, done something really bad.
Jingle bells, jingle bells, Santa, do you hear?
What a punishment! I promise I'll be good next year.

Because this journal is written specifically for nurses, those who are outside the profession may not understand or appreciate the humor. In fact, even some nurses have difficulty accepting the importance and need for laughter about our profession. Letters to the editor are published in each issue. One nurse expressed, "I am appalled, ...this is a crucial time for nursing. Many professionals are working diligently at demonstrating to the public the seriousness and importance of nursing. Now, you people are going to help our profession take several steps back by making fun of it. There is a time and place for laughing with one another, but publishing it is not the place! This will only serve to detract from the seriousness, critical analysis and professionalism of nursing" (Grant, 1991). This statement proves just how risky humor can be. What is funny to one person can be offensive to another. Different jokes for different folks!

Editor Doug Fletcher has remained committed to his vision of providing a humorous look at health care and recently published a book containing the "best of" JNJ from 1991-1993. It is entitled, *Whinorreha and Other Nursing Diagnosis*. He explains his philosophy about providing a humorous perspective on nursing: "Nurses should be able to enjoy their profession. The *Journal of Nursing Jocularity* was intended to look at the lighthearted side of our profession, and avoid the "terminal professionalism" that creeps in and squelches the ideals we once held as new grads. Because nursing is such a high stress profession, we have to publish humor that reflects the atmosphere prevalent in the nursing setting today. ... Because humor is one of our most powerful coping mechanisms, I feel that publishing gallows humor for health professionals is a risk we need to take. A humorless, burned-out nurse will be viewed as a heartless, cynical professional, and maybe even the proverbial battle-ax" (Fletcher, 1995, p. 113).

One nurse describes the importance of seeing the humorous side of our profession by saying, "I relax and laugh with other nurses to make it easier to laugh alone. Before I am through, I realize that for every earth-shattering problem in nursing, there is always a humorous counterpart!" (Storlie, 1965, p. 240).

Clowning Around For Nurses

I help nurses and patients laugh about their situations through my clown characters, "Nancy Nurse" and "Nurse Kindheart." You will learn more about their development later on in the book. "Nancy Nurse" is a wild and irreverent redhead with a combat belt full of tubes and equipment to "fight the war against disease." She is a "Nurse's Nurse" and nurses can relate to her, "get out of my way I've got work to do" attitude. "Nancy Nurse" says and does things to doctors, patients and supervisors that every nurse has wished she had the courage to do. Thank goodness for all of us that "real nurses" exercise more self restraint and maintain their composure and compassion. Nurses witness "Nancy's" clowning antics and experience a vicarious release of tension through laughter. "Nancy Nurse" provides coping humor.

"Nurse Kindheart" evolved as I began to entertain audiences of patients. As you might imagine, "Nancy Nurse" is a patient's worst nightmare of health-care reform gone berserk. I recognized that patients would be so agitated by this character that the therapeutic value of humor would be lost, so I created "Nurse Kindheart." She is a gentle, old fashioned, white-haired "traditional nurse." "Nurse Kindheart" as her name implies, is filled with compassion for the patient and will protect and comfort them through any situation. "Nurse Kindheart" provides hoping humor.

As a Nurse Humorist, I believe that humor is an essential part of healthcare. Patients and their families need it as much as professional caregivers. I carry this message to hospitals, patient support groups and communities through-out the U.S. and abroad. I promote the development of the therapeutic humor field by publishing articles in professional journals and coordinating professional networking efforts through the American Association for Therapeutic Humor (for information about membership, see the Humor Resource List). I encourage others to help their colleagues, patients and families develop humor skills to promote optimal health. This book has been created to take this message to an even larger audience: YOU, the reader! Whoever you are, whether health care professional, family caregiver, or just an interested bystander, be prepared to learn, laugh and heal with humor!

CHAPTER CHAT

NANCY NURSE: I guess a sense of humor involves more than just a whoopee cushion and a fresh pie in the face!

NURSE KINDHEART: Oh my yes, dear. Humor can help us to cope with many unpleasant realities.

NANCY NURSE: I heard that reality is the leading cause of stress! So a sense of humor would help get rid of that stress?

NURSE KINDHEART: Yes. And you'll be pleased to know, that the foundation of all humor begins with a sense of playfulness.

NANCY NURSE: That's where the pies and whoopee cushions come in!

NURSE KINDHEART: Not exactly dear. You see, humor is merely the ability to step back, look at your situation and use your imagination to create funny possibilities.

NANCY NURSE: Yeah, but some situations are just too serious to laugh about. You know, like cancer or death.

NURSE KINDHEART: Oh, I wouldn't be too sure about that. Sometimes, humor and laughter can help people survive. It gives them hope and courage. Hmmmm, that reminds me of a song (sung to the tune of, "You've Got to Have Heart"):

> "Oh you've got to have hope
> If your patient starts to mope
> Don't you worry, you just give 'em a grin
> So they won't give in and they can cope
> Cause ya gotta have hope!"

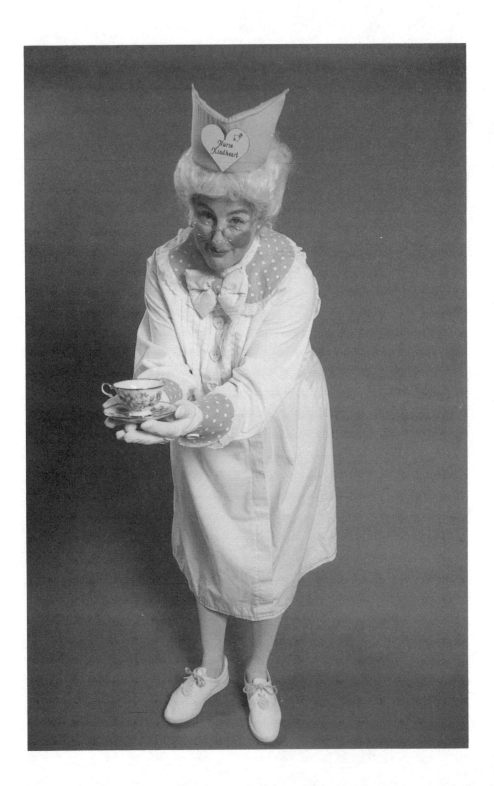

Chapter 2
The Caring Heart:
Service With a Smile

Laughing together can be a time of intimacy and communion,
a time when we come forward, fully present and touch into each other's
humanness and vulnerability. By joining in humor and acknowledging our
oneness, we can have a profound experience of unity and cooperation. That
in itself maybe one of the most profound expressions of
healing energy of which we are capable.

–Barry Sultanhoff, MD

Martha brought her eighty-four year old father to live with her when his Alzheimer's disease made it impossible for him to live safely in his own apartment. George had always been a stubborn and independent man, and the Alzheimer's disease seemed to intensify those qualities. He was able to manage most of his needs, like getting dressed and going to the toilet, but sometimes he got confused and his behavior became bizarre.

Early one morning, when Martha didn't find her father in his bed, she started to worry. As she walked down the hall, she noticed small pieces of constipated stool dotting the hallway into the kitchen. Rather than getting angry, she remembered the Hansel and Gretel fairy tale and said to herself, "Well, he just wanted to make sure he could find his way back to his room, so if I follow this trail he made, I'll be certain to find him at the other end." She did indeed find him in the living room with nothing on but his hat and shoes, holding his walking cane. Rather than explode with anger, she let herself be amused by how comical he looked. She asked him what he was planning to do. He said he was preparing to go for a walk. Calmly, she informed him that the elderly lady across the street was single and if he were to walk outside dressed as he was, as handsome as he is, she just might have a heart attack and die. George smiled and said he wouldn't want that to happen, and consented to wearing some clothes.

Martha could have responded to this situation with anger, but rather she chose to see the humor in it. First she "reframed" her situation and compared it to the fairy tale. Next, she allowed herself to be amused when she saw her father naked, and finally, she gave him a whimsical reason to put his clothes on. A humorous perspective gives us that new way of looking at the "same old problems" and provides possibilities for new solutions!

A sense of humor can help you overlook the unattractive, tolerate the unpleasant, cope with the unexpected, and smile through the unbearable.

—Moshe Waldoks

Caregiving vs Caretaking

Are you a caregiver? Caring has been described as an integral part of our survival and one of the oldest and most universal attributes of human culture (Leininger, 1981; Montgomery, 1993). Whether you are a professional, a family member, or a loving friend, caring for another person can be difficult. It can be frustrating, exhausting and discouraging. The latest statistics indicate that about fifteen percent of American adults are providing special care for seriously ill and aging relatives or friends at home. The average American woman spends seventeen years of her life caring for children, and eighteen years of her life helping aging parents (Sherman, 1995).

In the years ahead as health care continues to change, more of us will be caring for a relative or friend in the home. Family care providers often struggle with the demands of providing constant, around the clock care to their loved ones. In many ways, this is more difficult than providing professional care in a hospital setting. Professional caregivers work a defined number of hours and are relieved of their duties every eight to twelve hours to rest and care for themselves. Care is provided by a team of individuals, whereas in the home, there is usually only one or two people supplying care. Home care does not always provide the mechanism for much needed respites.

Do you "give care" to others or do you "take care" of others? Throughout this book I use the word "caregiver" because I want to capture a specific essence of this activity. Caregiving and caretaking are very different. *Caregiving* is authentic and is based on love; *caretaking* is dysfunctional and is based on fear. *Caretaking* behavior is characterized by: a need to control others and feel superior; feeling guilty when not helping others; and, a self-esteem based on approval from others. *Caregiving* behavior is characterized by: acting with compassion (suffering with, rather than suffering for); feeling humble; recognizing our own limitations and inadequacies; and, radiating joy with service (Summers, 1992).

How do families cope with the anxiety, frustrations, and fatigue of home care? How do they keep their hearts open and maintain their patience and compassion?

Compassion in Caregiving

Derived from the Latin "paticum," compassion means to suffer with someone and share in their fear, confusion, and anguish (Nouwen, 1980). It is the son who witnesses the helplessness of his mother who has a debilitating illness, and assures her of his unconditional love. Compassion is a sensitivity to the pain and suffering of the other (Fox, 1979). It is the husband who sits at the bedside of his wife, listening and comforting her while she cries about their stillborn child. Compassion compels us to be patient and kind with those we care for. It is the wife of the confused Alzheimers patient who carefully cleans up the plateful of food her husband threw on the floor, then prepares another and gently encourages him to eat.

How do these people find the grace and courage to continue caring despite the pain and frustration? Caring emanates from the depths of our human spirit and flows through the heart. Compassionate caregivers keep their hearts open and feel a loving connection with the human spirit. They understand the universal human condition: that we all wish to be free from pain and fear and live in peace and freedom. Compassion teaches us that peace and serenity do not lie in the absence of challenge, but rather in our capacity to face our hardships without judgment, prejudice or resistance (Kornfield, 1993).

True compassion does not ask for proof that our love makes a difference, nor does it seek approval or a reward for caring. As we establish a loving, spiritual connection with those we care for, the separation between self and other melts away. We begin to include ourselves in our compassion. If we hope to continue to care for others, we must remain sensitive to our own needs, intuitions and emotions. If we are focused only on caring for others, or pleasing them, or pacifying them, we will clearly not meet our own needs in the situation.

Compassion for ourselves gives rise to the power to transform resentment into forgiveness, hatred into friendliness and fear into respect for all beings.
It allows us to extend warmth, sensitivity, and openness to the sorrows around us in a truthful and genuine way.
The power of the compassionate heart, of genuine compassion, to transform the pain we encounter is extraordinary.

—Jack Kornfield

Providing enough time and energy to attend to our own needs requires that we set limits on the demands others place upon us. We must learn to say "No" without putting the other person out of our heart. By honoring ourselves; by establishing boundaries for what we can and cannot accept, we insure that we will have the strength and composure to continue as a caregiver. And, a sense of humor will help us keep our hearts open, our emotions calm, and our spirits high!

When you get to the end of your rope,
tie a knot and hang on. And swing!

—Leo Buscaglia

After her mother suffered a stroke, Jennifer made the decision to take her home to live with her. The medical preparation was easy compared to the preparation that was required in her heart. She purchased a special bed, educated herself about her mother's medications and the schedule, even supplied the spare bathroom with a toilet transferring device. But then came the hard part. How could Jennifer protect herself from the stress of living each day with her mother and this difficult, demanding condition? How could she cope and not give in to depression and frustration? What could she do to "keep it light"?

Humor and Caregiving

A sense of humor helps us to manage the stress of caregiving. The "detached perspective" that humor provides helps us to disengage from the suffering we witness and, yet, still remain sensitive. When we allow ourselves to laugh about our situation, we can accept our inadequacies and forgive ourselves. Laughter fills us with joy which we radiate to others. It allows us to rise above our difficulties and experience the beauty of life beyond the hardships of giving care. We transcend our everyday problems and feel optimistic and hopeful. Searching for humor, looking for something to laugh about, keeps us from focusing on the elements that are overwhelming or depressing.

It's the simple things we do, that we share with each other
and find funny... the common everyday things that
make us human. We see the absurdity in someone else,
that we know in ourselves... [we] feel connected.
This is the laughter of compassion.

—Arina Isaacson

Laughter and Stress Research

The stress and isolation of full-time caregiving can damage the health and well-being of the care provider. Studies have shown that caregivers are more likely than non-caregivers to experience depression, anxiety, and physical illness (Kiecolt-Glaser, et al., 1991). Research also indicates that people caring for a spouse with Alzheimer's, experience a decrease in their immune functioning and are more vulnerable to infections.

Dr. Janice Kiecolt-Glaser, a psychologist, and Dr. Ronald Glaser, an immunology researcher at the University of Ohio, looked at sixty-nine people who had been caring for a spouse with Alzheimer's for an average of five years. They compared the immune functions of these long-term caregivers with those of a group from the community, matched according to age, sex and income. The caregivers showed a decrease in three different immune measures: they had lower percentages of total T cells, helper T-cells, and the more closely the caregiver associated with the victim, the lower was his or her percentage of natural killer cells (NK). That's the bad news—the good news is, caregivers involved in a support group felt substantially less lonely and had significantly higher percentages of NK cells than those not involved with a support group (Butler, 1993; Cousins, 1989). Chapter Three provides further details about immune functions.

> Surveys have found that almost twenty-five percent of all primary caregivers have no one with whom they can discuss their physical, emotional or financial problems. Slightly less than half of the caregivers said their immediate families had no idea how much care they were giving. Considering the lack of people contact, it's not surprising that the rate of depression among caregivers is double that among non-caregivers of equivalent age, health and social status.
>
> —James Sherman

But wait—there is hope on the horizon! Research has found that an ability to laugh and find humor in our situations helps us adjust better to stress. Drs. Rod Martin and Herbert Lefcourt, formerly of the University of Waterloo in Ontario, gave fifty-six subjects four tests designed to measure the capacity to enjoy humor under a variety of circumstances. Three out of four tests showed that those who valued humor coped better with tension and stress. A subsequent study found that those who had the greatest ability to produce humor "on demand" were better able to counteract the negative emotional effects of stress (Martin & Lefcourt, 1983; Martin et al., 1988). A prescription for caregivers stating, "Laugh, every four hours, more if necessary" may be a lot healthier and a lot more fun than taking aspirin!!

Humor as a Nursing Intervention

Humor is one of 357 distinct nursing interventions identified by the Iowa Intervention Project which was designed to recognize the healing activities of nursing. Humor was operationally defined in this project as, "Facilitating the patient to perceive, appreciate and express what is funny, amusing or ludicrous in order to establish relationships, relieve tension, release anger, facilitate learning or cope with painful feelings" (McCloskey & Bulechek, 1992). What that says in plain English, is HUMOR HEALS!

Florence Nightingale, known as the "Lady with the Lamp," was the founder of modern nursing. I can see her now, walking through rows of cots in hospital tents near the Crimean battlefields, shining her light on the wounded, touching them briefly in the dark hours of the soul, as they struggled between life and death. Often it was her touch that moved something within them, some spark of will that grew into a desire to live (Shames, 1994). Accounts of her life indicate that Florence understood the power of humor. One of her patients noted, "What a comfort it was to see her pass by. She would speak to all, nod and smile... she was full of life and fun when she talked to us, especially if a man was a bit down hearted" (Kelly, 1981, p. 29).

As a Victorian woman, Florence was probably modest and refined in her choice of humor. I doubt that she donned a clown nose or a funny hat. Nevertheless, she gave her patients the gift of laughter, probably by telling a funny story or describing their situation in an amusing way. She also used humor in her communications with the war offices in England, trying to convince them to improve the conditions at the hospital camp. In one letter she wrote, "The vermin might, if they had but unity of purpose, carry off the four miles of beds on their backs and march them into the war office" (Kelly, 1981, p. 30).

Language of Laughter

The language of laughter connects people in an intimate way. Sometimes patients will use humor to communicate a concern, or enter into a serious discussion (Robinson, 1991; Gullickson, 1995). I remember the day I prepared a patient to go to the operating room for an orchiectomy (removal of the testicles). He was obviously nervous and there was fear in his eyes. As I prepped him, I wondered silently if he had been given any information about his surgery. My question was answered when he made a funny joke that expressed the root of his fear, "I guess after this is over I'll be a hen instead of a rooster!" He was probably too embarrassed to communicate his concerns directly, but they were obvious in his joking remark. I was then able to acknowledge his fears and provide him with information on what to expect and how it would affect his life. His little joke opened the door for me to connect with him and offer some stress-relieving education.

I'm reminded of another story about a nurse caring for an elderly woman with pneumonia, decubiti (pressure sores), and end-stage chronic brain syndrome. The patient had been reacting by screaming whenever she was touched. While changing her bed linens, the nurse began singing a song to relieve the stress of the patient's hysteria. The song was perfectly timed between the patient's screaming, on the silence of each deep breath!

Row, Row, Row your boat
Gently down the stream.
Fooled you. Fooled you.
I'm a submarine!

The patient stopped screaming and smiled in response to the song, listening for the next verse. And thus, a caring connection between the patient and nurse had been created with compassionate humor (Pedersen, 1987, p.19).

The Power of A Smile

No matter how grouchy you're feeling,
You'll find the smile more or less healing.
It grows in a wreath
All around the front teeth,
Thus preserving the face from congealing.

—Anthony Euwer

Most of us know that emotions have a physical response. When we are frightened, our hearts beat faster, our palms sweat and we tense up. There are also unique facial expressions associated with emotions. Have you ever wondered if it does any good to follow the advice of the old song and simply, "put on a happy face?"

According to Paul Ekman and Robert Levenson, psychologists from University of California, that advice may actually be true! They have discovered that facial expressions are universal across cultures and are linked neurologically to emotional states. Their research has shown that facial expressions are not only reactions to emotional states, but can provoke these states as well. In their study, subjects were not told what emotional state they were to supposed to portray, but instead were instructed to move certain muscle groups: pull their eyebrows down and together, and push their lower lip up, forming a facial expression that conveys anger in every human culture.

At the same time, the researchers measured the subjects' heart rate, finger temperature and muscle activity. Participants were asked to identify the feelings or sensations they experienced during each facial expression. Results showed that every emotional state is associated with specific physiological changes, and that these changes can be stimulated by facial expressions. The subjects' reported feelings that also matched their facial expressions (Ekman, 1984; Levenson, et al., 1990). Perhaps someday, patients will be scheduled for smile therapy!

> *Despair affects the immune system . . . I try to leave patients with something to smile about.*
>
> —Bernie Siegel, MD

Laughter and Tears

Laughing and crying often go together. They're both cathartic responses that serve to cleanse the body of distressing emotions. They provide an opportunity for people to communicate when they find themselves at the margins of their existence (Plessner, 1970).

As a hospice nurse, I visited a grieving family after the death of their loved one. Mary shared an unusual experience with me. "You know, after Richard died, I cried and cried, but my deepest tears remained trapped inside me. No matter what I did, I couldn't seem to release them. Then, about three weeks after the funeral, a couple came to visit me. All four of us used to go camping together every summer with our kids. We started remembering some of the funny things that had happened. One story struck me as particularly hilarious, and I started to laugh. The laughter got deeper and louder, I rocked back and forth, and tears began to flow. Gradually, before I knew it, I was crying. Then the crying turned to sobbing, and finally, my deepest tears that had been trapped for so long came pouring out. What a relief! After several minutes of sobbing, my crying began to subside. Just as I was almost finished, I started to smile as the tension subsided. The smile moved into a chuckle and soon I was laughing robustly and—joyously again."

Your joy is your sorrow unmasked. And the selfsame well from which your laughter rises was oftentimes filled with your tears. And how else can it be? The deeper that sorrow carves into your being, the more joy you can contain.

—Kahlil Gibran

More than two thousand years ago, Aristotle asserted that crying, "cleanses the mind." Today, modern research is proving he was right. At the Dry Eye and Tear Research Center in St. Paul, Minnesota, William Frey showed subjects a tear-jerker movie and collected their tears in a small test tube. A few days later, the same subjects returned and were again prompted to weep, this time by being exposed to the aroma of a cut onion. Frey discovered that the emotional tears contained more protein than the tears released as a result of the eye irritant. Both kinds contained stress chemicals, specifically adreno-corticotropic hormone (ACTH) which stimulates the release of adrenaline during stress, and leucine enkephalin, a morphine-like stress compound that may help mediate pain (Frey, 1985). So, go ahead and laugh till you cry, or cry till you laugh—it really is good for you!

Integrating Humor into the Plan of Care

Before we begin to apply humor in a therapeutic way, we must be prepared. First, we must understand our own sense of humor and our ability to laugh (self assessment). Next, we must evaluate the receptivity of the person with whom we wish to share our humor (consider the receiver). And, finally, we must devise a plan and select the type of humor that matches our own style and the needs of the patient (develop skills and resources).

Self Assessment

What value do you place on your own personal sense of humor? Do you really believe that humor is helpful? What makes you laugh? Once you understand what tickles your funny bone, you will be on your way to bringing more laughter into your life. Do you enjoy cartoons, jokes, toys, stand up comedy, amusing stories, being around funny people? Your sense of humor can help you cope with the stress of caregiving. A support group for caregivers may provide a community where you can discover what kind of humor appeals to you. Group members often share humorous stories and help others find the humor in difficult situations. It may be a safe place for you to develop your 'humor skills' especially, if you feel hesitant to use humor.

My own personal sense of humor has developed over many years. I grew up in a home filled with laughter. My father used to entertain our family with an endless variety of jokes and snappy one-liners. He was a salesman and used his jokes as a way to connect with his customers and build relationships. My mother, on the other hand, couldn't remember a joke to save her life. Well, that's not entirely true, she could remember about half the joke but would usually blow the punch line. Which of course, drove my father nuts! My mother did, however, have a wonderfully free and easy laugh. As a small child, I remember hearing my mother's laughter from the neighbor's house across the street. It was reassuring to hear, and we always knew where she was. As a teenager, however, I was absolutely mortified!

In elementary school I became the class clown because I loved to make people laugh. My third grade report card said, "Patty would be a good student if she'd only stop running around the room being silly all the time." Apparently, the school system was successful in containing my enthusiasm for comedy, because by high school I had become very shy and reserved. Fortunately my inner jester returned again when I started college, and helped me survive some very challenging times. I had entered UC Berkeley just as the free speech movement was starting and I remember crossing picket lines and dodging tear gas just to attend class. Our dormitory was filled with the sounds of raucous laughter as we released our tensions and fear.

It was in nursing school, however, that my sense of humor really began to develop. It was a survival tool. The freshman nursing students at UCSF Medical Center were grouped together and six of us shared our clinical experiences for the next three years. On our first clinical assignment, we were sent by bus to the VA Hospital in Menlo Park for a Psychiatric rotation. Our instructor took us to a locked ward filled with severely schizophrenic patients, some of whom had been there for ten to twenty years. She opened the locked door, ushered us inside, and after a brief twenty minute orientation, told us she would be back for us at 3 PM and left. We turned to face the thirty or so patients in the day room and witnessed some very strange behaviors. Some patients were pushing chairs back and forth across the room, others were actively hallucinating and arguing with invisible people, still others sat in chairs with their hands down their pants, rocking back and forth and moaning.

We were only nineteen years-old, and nothing in our lives had prepared us for this moment. As I look back on it now, I realize it was we students who received the shock therapy that day. We looked at each other in desperation and promised to help one another survive the experience. Well, we did survive and continued to return each Wednesday for the rest of the semester. And, how did we survive? Through laughter, of course. Each day, on the bus ride back to San Francisco, we shared our adventures, imitated the patients, planned outrageous responses to their bizarre behaviors and basically just laughed and laughed, so hard sometimes that we wet our pants.

We continued to laugh our way through three years of nursing school, helping each other see the comedy and cope with the tragedy. We all grew up and turned out to be pretty fine nurses. I have continued to laugh with my nursing colleagues, my patients and the whole healthcare team for the last twenty-five years, and its the best way I could survive (see: Kramer, 1974).

Over the years, my appreciation for comedy continued to grow and develop. I went to clown school during another challenging time in my life. I was struggling to accept a divorce that I didn't want, adjusting to life as a single mother of a small baby, and working in an ICU for brain injured patients. My clown, my inner jester, saved my mental health, if not my life. Years later, I brought my clown and my appreciation of humor together, and developed a workshop for nurses called "Jest for the Health of It.™" (see, Humor Resource List). More recently, I've tailored my message to reach patients, families, corporations, educators and pedestrians. My goal is to help people recognize, develop and apply their sense of humor to survive the challenges in their own lives. You might say I've come full circle back to that little third grade girl, running around the room acting silly all the time, but now, I'm the teacher!

Consider The Receiver

Your attempts at humor will be more likely to stimulate laughter if you begin with an understanding of your care receiver's sense of humor. Some interesting research has shown that the people you communicate with, will take in seven percent of your words, thirty-eight percent of your vocal characteristics and fifty-five percent of your nonverbal signals (Sherman, 1995, p. 70). Now, from a clown's perspective, let me tell you how these statistics "play out" when you want to make 'em laugh.

"Nancy Nurse" and "Nurse Kindheart" have learned the art of reading an audience. Recently, they got together, considered these statistics and have developed a "plan of care." Let me share their wise advice, based on their professional experience. If you too, want to make 'em laugh, consider their wisdom:

- ♥ Your patient will notice less than ten percent of your words, so choose them carefully. Develop a collection of zingy one-liners, clever riddles, funny stories, and brilliant jokes for every occasion. Learn to tell a joke: Pause occasionally as you deliver the material; create a brief and concise set-up for the punch line; pause before delivering the punch line; speak the punch line clearly and with "punch!" (Helitzer, 1987; Bates, 1995; Carter, 1989; Goldberg, 1991; see Appendix).

- ♥ Vocal characteristics are five times more important than your words alone. Try to change the pace and tone of your voice or speak with an accent, and your words will have more impact.

♥ The most powerful communication tool we have is our ability to communicate non-verbally. Facial expressions, physical gestures, costuming, props, the way we walk or stand or reach for something, are non-verbal communication tools that provide the greatest impact on our audience (Stolzenberg, 1981; Fife, 1988; Pipkin, 1989).

Assess your patient's "Funny bone." Consider these questions as you select the humor style you wish to use (Herth, 1984).

♥ Has your patient given you any clues that indicate they are receptive to humor?

Perhaps you have heard them laugh while reading or watching TV. Listen for the sounds of laughter when friends come to visit or call on the phone. Do they attempt to share humor? If they share a joke, a funny card or a cartoon that made them laugh, these may indicate they are open and receptive to humor.

George was a patient in our Coronary Care Unit after a nearly fatal heart attack. He was recovering slowly, but was having difficulty adjusting to the mandatory "bed rest." Using the bedpan was particularly embarrassing for him. One day after he'd opened his mail, he excitedly called me into his room, announcing, "I thought you might learn something from this." He handed me the card which had two cartoons entitled, 'Proper and Improper Techniques for Administering the Bedpan.'

The first cartoon showed the nurse with one hand under the patients' back, gently lifting him while she slid the bedpan underneath with the other. The next cartoon showed the nurse lifting the patient up by the penis. He grinned at me and winked, "Just thought you might need a reminder." For the next few days, whenever he needed the bedpan, he'd ask me, "Now, you do remember the proper technique, don't you?" We always chuckled and I'm sure it helped him cope with the embarrassment.

♥ What is your patients' ability to perceive and understand humor?

> Consider any hearing, visual, mental, or reading deficits. For humor to stimulate laughter, we must first "get the gag." We must hear the joke, see the funny prop, or read and understand the humor in an amusing story.

> If your patient is deaf, they may have difficulty responding to jokes or audio tapes of comic routines. Obviously, the visual humor contained in costumes, signs, cartoons or silent films would be more appropriate for a deaf patient. If your patient is visually impaired, you may need to use larger props, such as a gigantic stethoscope or a comical crab hat.

> Some humor is dependent upon astute cognitive skills or the ability to understand clever associations and word play. People with Alzheimer's, brain damage, or mental illness may have trouble comprehending the intricate humor of a complex story or joke. Playful physical comedy such as clown antics or sheer buffoonery may be perceived as funnier (Nahemow, 1986).

> Kathy Passanisi, a physical therapist and now a full-time humor speaker, tells of the time she wore her large, red, foam crab hat into the nursing home. Rose, an elderly resident saw her walk by and asked about it. Kathy told her, "I'm just feeling a little crabby today." Rose agreed that she was feeling crabby, too. Kathy offered her the hat to wear and Rose accepted. The rest of the day, Rose sat in the hallway announcing to people that passed by, "I'm feeling a little crabby today." Her crabby mood gradually dissolved with all the smiles she received.

♥ How does the patient use humor?

> Observe the kind of humor your patient chooses to create. Does it seem to be a natural part of their lifestyle? Are they physically playful

or mentally witty? Are they storytellers? Do they utilize sarcastic, cynical humor? Or is their humor warm and gentle? Do they interact with their surroundings in a playful, childlike way?

I was having dinner with my family and discussing some of my frustrations at work. I must admit, I started whining, not loudly mind you, just a sort of constant droning that makes people uneasy. You would have thought I was the president of the BMW club: Bitching, Moaning and Whining (Schultz, 1991; Farley, 1995). About midway through the meal, my 10 year-old son Ken, picked up the spoon as if it were a microphone and announced, "Now hear this, now hear this: Mom is really fed up and irritable. Proceed with caution!" It was so funny, we all laughed, and I got the message loud and clear, "We understand how you feel, Mom and we'll try to be sensitive."

♥ Are there any humorous topics the patient might consider taboo?

Be cautious of using humor that might offend someone. People are most easily offended by humor centered around religion, sexuality, racism, and politics. Observe the kind of humor your patient responds to or shares with you. This will give you some clues about their sensibilities and limits. Remember, always be sincere when sharing humor. If the joke is offensive to you, how can you share it in a humorous manner? Humor is risky business. It is easy to offend someone if you are not conscious of their sensitivities. Let that guide you in your choice of material.

Genuine humor is always kindly and gracious.
It points out the weakness of humanity, but shows
no contempt and leaves no sting.

—Author Unknown

♥ Do you find your patient has a preference for a particular type of humor?

> Some people enjoy a witty pun or a play on words (Hauptman, 1988; Lederer, 1991). Comedian Gallager asks, "Why is it that we park in the driveway and drive on the parkway?" Joel Goodman's *Laughing Matters* magazine is one of the punniest humor resources I've ever seen. He uses clever wordplay to create intriguing titles for articles and special interest sections, like these:
>
> > Grin and Share It.
> > Fun-liners Jest for You.
> > Playing with a Fool deck.
> > Reader's Di-Jest: Wisdom and Witdom from You, the Readers.
>
> Your patient may like cartoons and have favorite ones they look for in the daily newspaper. People have preferences for humorous authors that can tickle their funny bone such as Dave Barry, Erma Bombeck, Mark Twain, or Dorothy Parker. Toys and games will get some folks giggling. Be careful to choose a style of humor that the person already enjoys. As trust and comfort levels build, you can introduce other styles of your own.

♥ Do they prefer a certain comedy artist?

> Comic artists have as distinct a style in their comical images, as Rembrandt, Monet, and Picasso have in their works of art. If we look to films, television, standup comics, and clowning, we find diverse styles, all of which create laughter. Consider the differences in style between Lucille Ball and Roseanne Arnold, Robin Williams and Groucho Marx, or clowns like, Lou Jacobs and Emmett Kelly. Most people are intolerant of constant "put down humor." Comedy can be subtle, outrageous, intellectual, or slapstick, so audience preference is important to consider when introducing humor into the plan of care.

Different jokes for different folks.

Joel Goodman

♥ Will the humor be perceived as annoying? Will it indicate caring?

> The Hippocratic oath advises medical doctors, "Above all else, do no harm." We as Mirth Directors (MD's) must also heed this advice. If in doubt—hold out! Become aware of the subtle cues a patient gives you in response to your initial humorous attempts. Watch their eyes. Do they become alert and shining? Or do they furrow their brows and look away? Is the laughter you hear sincere or merely a polite response to fill the silence?

> Listen to the tonal quality of their laugh. The high pitched "TeeHee," which seems to come out the top of the head, may indicate tension and nervousness. The hollow "HehHeh," from the throat, may indicate a polite but insincere response. A more hearty "HaHa," coming from the heart space, indicates a real enjoyment of the humor. Finally, a robust and booming "HoHoHo," from the belly, usually indicates a deep appreciation of the humor and an eagerness to laugh.

♥ Ask yourself if you may be laughing at the patient or their situation before they give you permission to poke fun.

> This is the aspect of *timing.* If we insert humor about personal aspects of a patients' life or things they consider to be private, they will feel offended or deeply hurt. When you do make a mistake (and we all do, sooner or later) first, forgive yourself for being obtuse or insensitive, then make amends with the patient.

Develop Skills And Resources - Filling Your Toolbox

As you begin to apply humor therapeutically, it is important to collect a variety of tools and resources. You may decide to use all or some of the

suggestions given below. You may find others you like better. Let your
personal preference be your guide. Use the Humor Resource List at the end
of this book for some valuable references for humor tools. And most of all, be
sure to have fun while you fill your toolbox!

♥ Create a scrapbook of cartoons.

> Place the cartoons in a photo album with peel back pages. This will
> protect and keep them clean. Consider the audience that will read
> this scrapbook. If it's for an outpatient waiting room, try to find
> humor about the situation these people will be facing. You'll find one
> of the best selections of humor about patients, doctors, and nurses in
> the seven volumes of Herman cartoons (Unger, 1989). Be careful not
> to add any potentially offensive or shocking items to the scrapbook.
> Include a variety of cartoon artists. If you are preparing this collection
> for a family member, you will have greater awareness of their humor
> style and their limits.

> Some of the cartoons with a more universal appeal include: *Ziggy,
> Family Circle, Peanuts, Garfield, Farcus, Frank and Earnest,* and,
> *Herman.* Others cartoons that have a bit more pointed appeal are,
> *Dilbert, The FarSide, Callahan, Cathy* and *Doonesbury.* And, some of
> the cartoonists that are particularly funny to healthcare professionals
> are, John Wise, Tom Jackson, and Brian Moench. All of these cartoon-
> ists are listed in the Humor Resource List, Appendix, or Bibliography.

> A cartoon by John Wise shows the back side of a patient wearing a
> hospital gown, with the patient's buttocks showing. The caption
> reads, "Now I know why they call it ICU." A cartoon by Brian
> Moench is entitled, "Nightmare before Surgery." Three people in
> surgical scrubs are looking down at the patient, and the first has a
> cleaver behind her back and she says, "Hi, I'm Lorena Bobbit and I'll
> be assisting with your surgery." The next person says, "Hi, I'm Jack
> Kevorkian, I'll be your anesthesiologist." And, the last person looks

down and says, "Hello, I'm Hillary Rodham Clinton, and NO, you may not choose your own doctor."

♥ Develop a file of funny jokes, stories, greeting cards, bumper stickers, poems and songs.

When you hear something funny write it down immediately, before you forget! Many humorous resources are available on the Internet. Books of jokes are available in stores and libraries, but I find these to be rather unreliable resources for usable material. They are often offensive, dated, or just not funny to me. A better method to build your collection is to write down jokes you hear from friends, see on television, or read in magazines. Reader's Digest is a great suppository (excuse me, repository!) of humorous jokes, stories and observations.

♥ Collect or borrow funny books, videos and audio tapes of comedy routines.

These can be found in libraries, humor sections of book stores, mail order catalogs, or at humor conferences. Perhaps your caregiver support group or hospital library should have these resources available to loan?

Some of my favorite comedy videos are, "King of Hearts" with Alan Bates, and "The Long Long Trailer" with Lucille Ball. The comedy styles are dramatically different. The film with Lucy is slapstick. Lucy is in the trailer while Ricky drives down a winding mountain road. She is attempting to prepare a meal, but as the trailer swings from one side of the road to the other, she is tossed about and the food spills everywhere. Her expressions of exasperation are priceless.

"King of Hearts" is a film about an American soldier who is sent into a small French town to warn the citizens of an impending attack by the Germans. He is knocked out for brief period during which time the citizens flee the city, the Germans march in, find it empty and leave. In the midst of all this, the people from the local insane asylum escape and return to the empty town and to their former professions.

Bates, the American soldier, regains consciousness and enters the town to warn the citizens, which unbeknownst to him are the escapees from the asylum. The citizens' behaviors are bizarre, but their hearts are warm and loving. A series of comical encounters unfold.

♥ Keep a file of local clowns, magicians, storytellers, and puppeteers.

Invite them to entertain at your facility, the patients' home, or for a group function. The Humor Resource List in this book will help you find clown associations in your community. Guidelines for hospital performing are included in Chapter 4 and Chapter 5. As I travel around the country presenting my "Jest for the Health of It! ™" workshops, hospitals frequently schedule "Clown Rounds" at their facilities. "Nurse Kindheart" visits the patients and nurses throughout the hospital and brings the magic of laughter to the bedside.

♥ Collect toys, interactive games, noise makers, and squirt guns.

Keep them available to play with. If you will be sharing these toys with a patient, keep in mind safety and cleanliness factors.

Squirt guns are great for patients who have some hostility to release— let them "shoot" at the nurses. Caution should be taken that water does not puddle on the floor creating a safety hazard and patients' should be instructed not to aim for the face.

Small wind up toys can be fun to play with. I have a pair of shoes that walk around when wound up and a large nose that does the same.

♥ Create a humor journal or logbook to record funny encounters or humorous discoveries.

On days when you really need a laugh, but can't seem to find anything funny, you will have a collection of amusing stories at your fingertips. A nurse in one of my workshops told me about creating a journal for the operating room where she worked. She called the book, *The Days of Our Knives,* and here is one of her stories:

One day a nurse walked through the area where patients were waiting to go into the operating room and overheard a husband ask his wife, "What does that sign, 'NPO' on your bed mean? The patient lifted the sheet, looked underneath, and then replied, "Well, Henry, I think it means, "No Panties On."

♥ Establish a bulletin board in your facility or on your refrigerator at home to post cartoons, bumper stickers and funny signs.

If the display is public you must consider the sensitivities of the audience and be careful to exclude potentially offensive (ageist, sexist, racist) material. I've seen refrigerator magnets with messages like these,

Never eat more than you can lift .
My Karma Ran Over My Dogma.
I'm not PMS, I really am a Bitch.

I worked in one hospital where we placed a dry-erase drawing board in the nurses bathroom. We taped up a photograph of every staff physician's face. Nurses could then "doodle" and draw their interpretation of the neck down portion. The images we drew depended upon the physician's demeanor and personality.

♥ Subscribe to a humorous newsletter or journal to collect new ideas and inspiration. Some of my favorites include, *Journal of Nursing Jocularity, Laughing Matters, LaughMakers, Funny Times, Therapeutic Humor, Laughter Prescription,* and *Humor and Health Journal.* There are many others as well. For an extensive list consult Ellenbogen's, *The Directory of Humor Magazines and Humor Organizations in America and Canada* listed in the Bibliography of this book.

As I was browsing through my latest *Journal of Nursing Jocularity,* I came upon a list of suggested songs that hospitals could play over the public address system, as a kind of "secret code" to the staff, informing them of what was occurring in other parts of the hospital. A few years ago, many hospitals started playing a fifteen second segment of "Brahms' Lullaby" whenever a baby was born. This was wonderfully therapeutic for the staff because it offered a gentle reminder that "good news" was happening at that moment. This is a list of imaginary songs that other departments could request to honor their "events."

> Grand mal Seizure - "Shake, Rattle and Roll"
> Respiratory Distress - "I'm Mister Blue"
> Colonoscopy - "Bad Moon Rising"
> Preventing your Patient from Coding - "You Say Good-bye, I Say Hello"
> Eye Surgery - "I Can See Clearly Now"
> End of Visiting Hours - "Hit the Road Jack"

♥ Educate yourself about therapeutic humor.

> Attend conferences, workshops, and conventions. More effective techniques are developed daily. New research is published, and better resources are available on a regular basis. Stay up-to-date in this rapidly growing field. A list of associations that produce humor conferences are included in the Humor Resource List of this book.

As you embark upon this journey into therapeutic humor, remember you may have to create the map as you go along. Each individual and situation is unique and the terrain will change from day to day. Travel lightly and be prepared to change directions if needed. Most of all, have fun along the way!

CHAPTER CHAT

NURSE KINDHEART: It's so pleasing to know that Florence Nightingale, the founder of modern nursing, helped her patients to laugh.

NANCY NURSE: Hey, isn't she the one they called the "Lady with the Lamp?" Maybe that was part of her message, you know, helping everyone "lighten up!"

NURSE KINDHEART: Perhaps my dear. Being a caregiver or a care receiver can feel like a heavy burden, and if we can lighten the situation in any way, everyone will feel some relief.

NANCY NURSE: I try to help my patients to laugh by wearing funny rubber noses. Other times I tell silly jokes and riddles. But, you know, some patients don't think that's very funny. They don't laugh at all!

NURSE KINDHEART: Well now, you must remember: Different Jokes for Different Folks. Some people prefer an amusing story, others like to look at cartoon books, and some enjoy watching a stand up comic. You've got to know your audience.

NANCY NURSE: I found a great variety of ideas in this chapter, and I took a peak at Chapter 4. There's even more ideas there. Yahoo! Let's get readin'!

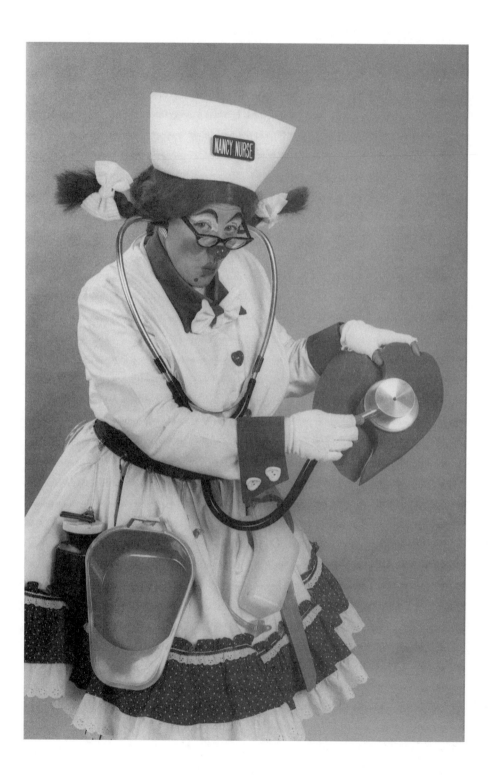

Chapter 3
The Healing Heart:
Medical Mirth

Laughter serves as a blocking agent. Like a bullet-proof vest,
it may help protect you against the ravages of negative emotions
that can assault you in disease.

—Norman Cousins

Have you ever heard someone comment, "He worried himself sick," or "She died of a broken heart," or the familiar, "Laughter is the best medicine." These commonly used expressions reflect the belief that thoughts and emotions affect our health. Modern scientific research into the mind-body connection explains how this is possible. In this Chapter we explore the communication mechanisms between the mind (thoughts and feelings) and the body (health and disease). We examine how the body responds to excessive stress and how laughter is the perfect antidote!.

I have a scientific mind and enjoy reading research reports. Seeing charts, graphs and statistically relevant data, excites me (really!). Some people are bored to death by scientific details, but they are interested in the general concepts and findings of the studies. In this Chapter, I will provide something for everybody. I will begin by introducing you to some of the pioneers of humor research, and then give a brief overview of humor studies which have been published over the last ten years.

Pioneers

Humor is a relatively new area of medical inquiry. Not surprisingly, serious laughter research has only been conducted since the 1960's. Most of the 'pioneers' in humor research are still alive and active in the field today. Dr. Vera Robinson, nurse and Professor Emeritus of the School of Nursing at California State University at Fullerton, completed her doctoral research on the importance of humor for the health professional. She has written one of the first textbooks about humor in nursing, *Humor and the Health Professions* (Robinson, 1991). Dr. William F. Fry Jr., psychiatrist and Professor Emeritus at Stanford University, was one of the first researchers to explore the importance of humor as a communication tool in family therapy (Wooten, 1994a). He went on to design physiological studies that measure the effects of laughter on the cardiovascular and respiratory system (Fry, 1971; Fry, 1986).

Norman Cousins, journalist and editor of the *Saturday Review,* used laughter to facilitate his recovery from a degenerative collagen disease. In his book, *Anatomy of an Illness,* he captured the attention of both the medical and lay communities when he discussed the possible health benefits of laughter. Cousins inspired others to examine the healing powers of humor, and reported some early research results in his second book, *Head First—The Biology of Hope.*

Other trailblazers include psychologists Herbert Lefcourt and Rod Martin, whose studies focused on the ability of humor to moderate the emotional response to stress. Their landmark book, *Humor and Life Stress: Antidote to Adversity,* was published in 1986 and is regarded as a standard reference book in humor research. Ronald Glaser, an immunologist and Janice Kiecolt-Glaser, a psychologist from the University of Ohio, have examined the effect of stress on the immune system. They have published numerous articles discussing their research on patients with AIDS, spousal caregivers, students facing exams, and many other people coping with difficulties. Lee Berk and Stanley Tan, immunology researchers from Loma Linda University Medical Center, have completed the most significant research to date about the impact of laughter on the immune system.

Inquiring Minds Want to Know

The process of scientific inquiry is well defined. It begins with questions that have no obvious answers. Next, the known facts are gathered and reviewed. Then, a hypothesis is formulated to express our suspicions about the truth. After our formulations are completed, research techniques and methods are established, implemented, and the results are measured. Based on the measured results, conclusions are drawn that will either prove or disprove the hypothesis. Let's apply this process of inquiry to humor and laughter and their possibilities of enhancing our health.

Questions

Does a sense of humor help us cope with stressful events in our lives? Can humor and laughter stimulate changes in the body that will enhance health and facilitate recovery from illness?

Review Of The Facts

Excessive, unrelenting stress can lead to illness (Selye, 1956; Dohenwend & Dohrenwend, 1974; Selye, 1974; Dohenwend & Dohrenwend, 1981). Stress can weaken the immune system (Solomon, 1981; Palmblad, 1981; Irwin et al., 1987), and predispose one to infection or even cancer (Temoshok, 1992; Solomon, 1985; Soloman, 1987). But, humor and laughter can mitigate the effects of stress and aid in our recovery from illness (Berk & Tan, 1989; Berk & Tan, 1993; Kiecolt-Glaser, et al, 1987a; Kiecolt-Glaser, et al, 1991) which Norman Cousins demonstrated successfully in his own healing (Cousins, 1979).

Hypothesis

Humor will modify our emotional response to stress. Humor will stimulate our immune system.

Methods And Results

Lefcourt and Martin (1986) studied fifty-six psychology students. The subjects completed several tests which measured recent life changes; negative mood states; and the ability to use and appreciate humor. Their research results indicated that a person with a strong sense of humor has significantly lower negative mood shifts when life changes occur, than a person with a weak sense of humor. Similar research conducted by Nezu (1988), but using different tools, confirmed these findings.

This I believe to be the chemical function of humor:
to change the character of our thought.

—Lin Yutang

Lee Berk and Stanley Tan have published research showing that the immune system is stimulated and strengthened during the experience of mirthful laughter (Berk & Tan, 1988). In a carefully controlled study, they examined the immune response of medical students who viewed a video performance of the comedian Gallager, the Sledge-o-matic Man. Blood samples were analyzed before, during, and after the comedy routine. A control group that did not experience the humorous intervention were used for comparison. One of their findings revealed that serum cortisol levels decreased significantly in the group experiencing laughter. Cortisol levels are known to increase during the experience of stressful emotions, when the brain signals the adrenal gland to produce corticosteroids which will increase blood sugar and decrease the immune response. Their findings support the hypothesis that laughter keeps our immune system strong, which in turn, keeps us healthy.

This research team also recorded increased activity in natural killer cells in the participants' response to laughter (Berk & Tan, 1989a). Natural killer cells release a substance that destroys tumor cells and deadly viruses. Among cancer patients, reduced natural killer cell activity is associated with an increase in the spread of tumors (Levy et al., 1985). Hang on to this thought, as the importance of each of these immune parameters will be explained later in this chapter. In addition to increased activity in natural killer cells, the number of helper T-cells increased in response to laughter. The helper/suppresser ratio also increased. This finding is significant, because helper T-cells are essential in mobilizing many immune cells. This is especially helpful in the battle against AIDS, as the AIDS virus is known to attack the helper T-cell.

Since AIDS emerged as a recognized disease in the early 1980's, news of its virulence has been grim. Yet, there are many cases of long term survivors, living seven years and longer after diagnosis. Psychiatrist George Soloman became interested in this group and studied the attitudes and personalities of these survivors. While his findings relate to a small number of patients, the results are important for any patient or survivor of illness. Solomon found that many AIDS survivors had unfulfilled commitments in life as well as plans for the future. They saw their illness as a challenge rather than a threat. Many reached out to offer support to other AIDS patients. Most of the long-term survivors had people in their life they could talk to about their fears and concerns. At the same time, they were sensitive to their own physical and psychological needs and could withdraw from outside commitments and care for themselves when necessary (Solomon, 1987).

Conclusions

Research has shown that a strong sense of humor can balance our negative mood shifts when life events force us to change (Lefcourt, 1986; Nezu et al., 1988). Different emotions stimulate a variety of chemical secretions from our brains. These chemicals (neurotransmitters) carry messages to the immune cells and may cause the cells to change their behavior or effectiveness. This reminds me of the old computer term, "GIGO—garbage in, garbage out." To keep healthy, think, "HIHO—Happy in, happy out!"

*The chemicals that are running our body and our brain
are the same chemicals that are involved in emotion.
And that says to me that... we'd better pay more attention
to emotions with respect to health.*

—Candace Pert

How the Idea for Laughter Research Began

Norman Cousins enlightened the medical community about the healing potential of laughter in his book, *Anatomy of an Illness*. In 1968, Cousins was diagnosed with ankylosing spondylitis, a potentially life-threatening, degenerative disease of the collagen tissue. Collagen is a substance found in the connective tissue of the body which is essential in holding the cells and larger structures of the body together. Cousin's case was so extreme that he soon experienced great difficulty and pain moving his joints. He was told that his prospect for recovery was very bleak. Because of discomfort and fatigue, he was unable to travel or play tennis, activities which brought him great joy and satisfaction.

Cousins refused to accept his grim prognosis, and decided to take charge of his own treatment, working in partnership with his physician. He remembered reading about the adverse consequences of negative emotional states on the chemical balance of the body.

He reasoned that, if negative emotions played any part in predisposing him to illness, then perhaps positive emotions would aid in his recovery. He sought activities that increased his positive emotions, such as faith, hope, festivity, determination, confidence, joy and a strong will to live. And he knew that laughter helped create positive emotions. With this in mind, Cousins watched films of the Marx Brothers and Candid Camera. He had nurses read to him from humorous books. He played practical jokes and told jokes. And, lo and behold—he began feeling better. Blood tests showed that his sedimentation rate (an index of the degree of infection or inflammation in the body) decreased after his laughter sessions, and continued to fall, as he gradually recovered.

After several months of this "humor therapy," his illness resolved and never bothered him again. One could argue that Cousins would have recovered anyway, even without the laughter. Or one could say, that the results were not scientifically significant and represent the observations of a single case. However, Cousins continued his quest to understand just how his healing occurred.

Cousins spent the remaining twelve years of his life as an Adjunct Professor at UCLA Medical School where he established a "Humor Task Force" to coordinate and support clinical research about laughter (Cousins, 1989). Today, twenty-five years after Cousins' self-healing experience with laughter, we have the scientific research to support the specific physiological changes which his individual story suggested. Cousins believed that the onset of his illness was caused by excessive stress. He believed that if he had practiced 'stress and humor management' earlier, he might not have become ill in the first place.

Stress Defined

Stress is a word that is used in a variety of ways to talk about a series of events and responses. People talk about stress as if it were a feeling, "I feel stressed." Others imply that stress is an ambiance or circumstance, as, "He has a lot of stress at work." Stress, as defined in terms of physics, is the force exerted by any one thing against another. All of these definitions include qualities of tension, pressure, and resistance.

I feel like my body turns into one big knot when I get stuck in traffic on the way to a meeting! This morning when I left for work, I was relaxed and well rested, eager to share my ideas at a staff meeting. Then, I'm stuck on the freeway, in the middle of hundreds of cars. The hands of the clock move forward and I don't. My mind races ahead, my engine idles. I begin to imagine all the problems that will arise because of my absence. My hands clench the steering wheel, my neck and shoulders become tense, I start to sweat. I am no longer relaxed, rested or eager to share. I am tense, agitated and closed. I am STRESSED!

Stress And Imbalance

Stress is a necessary part of life. People cannot maintain an erect posture without the stress and tension of opposing muscles that balance each other and keep the skeletal system erect. Eating puts some stress on the digestive system, and exercise puts stress on the cardiovascular system. This essential stress is beneficial and promotes balance in our bodies. But it is the daily, prolonged, unrelieved stress that upsets the body's well-being. Worrying about the meeting I missed when I was stuck in traffic triggered an emotional response that is described as "fight or flight."

Harvard physiologist, Walter Cannon, defined "fight or flight" as the automatic response of all animals (including humans) when they perceive a threat to their life. The body changes with dramatic suddenness, and prepares to run away or fight:

Body Response to Stress

- ♥ Heart rate increases, blood pressure rises to pump blood quickly to the necessary tissues, carrying oxygen and nutrients to cells.
- ♥ Breathing becomes rapid and shallow.
- ♥ Epinephrine is released from the adrenal gland causing blood flow to hands and feet to diminish. This protects you from bleeding to death quickly if you are injured during the fight or flight.
- ♥ Pupils dilate to let in more light; hearing and smell improve.
- ♥ Liver releases stored sugar into the blood to meet the increased energy demands. Blood sugar rises.
- ♥ Body sweats to cool itself, since increased metabolism generates more heat.

♥ Adrenal gland releases corticosteroids which decrease the immune response, so we don't have an allergic reaction to the dust kicked up during the fight or flight.

Any event which we believe is threatening or exciting creates a "fight or flight" response. A roller coaster ride will produce these changes. Simply anticipating a tense event can trigger the stress response and throw us out of balance. Stage fright or anxiety about a job interview will trigger some of these changes. While missing a Staff meeting is far from life threatening, we call the emotions we experience, STRESS.

Stress Response - Selye Theory

Pioneer researcher, Hans Selye, described stress as an event which creates an upset in the body's balance, or homeostasis. As part of Selye's theory, he formulated a three part view of how the stress response works. In the initial *(alarm)* stage, a stressor is recognized and metaphorical alarms go off in your head, telling you that you are in danger, or threatened in some way.

John opened his eyes sleepily and peered at his alarm clock. It blinked back 8:30 AM. "Oh no!" The alarm didn't go off and now he would be late for work. He quickly dressed, ran to the car and sped down the street. A small child ran out from between two parked cars and John slammed on his brakes, hit the horn and swerved. The child, physically unharmed, began to shriek and cry. The child's mother came running outside screaming about John's reckless driving. He resented being blamed for something that was not his fault, but he was also grateful that the child was not hurt.

He finally reached the freeway and thought he'd only be an hour late to work. John became preoccupied thinking about how upset his boss would be, maybe he'd be fired. His company had recently experienced many cutbacks, and he felt lucky to have a job. What if he did get fired? Who would hire a fifty-three year-old marketing rep? How would he survive, he couldn't retire yet. As he worried and fretted, he could feel a knot growing in his stomach. Suddenly, some jerk cut in front of him and John almost slammed into the back of his truck. Angry and annoyed, he blasted his horn and started yelling, his heart was pounding so loudly, he could hear it inside his head. By the time John arrived at work, his shirt was soaked in sweat and he had a splitting headache. Though his alarm clock had remained silent, John had experienced several alarm stages of the stress response.

The second stage is *adaptation or resistance,* which comes with the successful mobilization of the stress response system and the reattainment of homeostatic balance.

When John awoke and leapt out of bed, his peripheral vascular system adapted to this sudden change of position and constricted to prevent him from becoming dizzy or passing out. It relaxed again after he was up and about. When John quickly responded to avoid hitting the small boy, his heart rate increased; his blood pressure rose; his neck and shoulders became tense; his blood was shunted away from his gastrointestinal tract; epinephrine surged into his blood stream which increased his alertness and made his heart pound even harder; glycogen (complex stored sugar) was released from his liver, requiring his pancreas to secrete insulin, to move the sugar back into the cells and convert into energy so that his blood sugar would normalize. Gradually John's muscles relaxed and his heart rate and blood pressure dropped, but soon after that, his burst of anger caused all of the physical changes to occur again, this time with an increase in gastric acid secretion.

After prolonged stress, the body enters the third stage, which Selye termed exhaustion. This is where stress-related diseases develop.

If this scene were to be repeated frequently, John's body would simply wear out. His adrenal gland would weaken, as would his liver, pancreas, and heart. Eventually, John would begin to complain of stomach pain, tension headaches, fatigue, high blood pressure, diarrhea, irregular heart rate, chest pains, dermatitis, insomnia, frequent colds, depression or anxiety. The current belief is not that the stress response runs out, but rather, with prolonged activation, the stress response itself becomes damaging. It is this critical concept that underlies the emergence of much stress related disease (Benner, 1989; Sapolsky, 1994).

You know what happens when you get angry?
First, your face gets just like a fist. Then your heart
gets like a bunch of bees that fly up and sting your brain
in the front. Your eyes are like two dark clouds
looking for trouble. Your blood is like a tornado.
And then you have bad weather inside your body.

—by Jane Wagner "Edith Ann"

Stress – The Good News and The Bad News

Stress can improve our cognitive and sensory skills. When faced with a stressful situation, our memory improves and our senses become sharper. We become like animals threatened with harm. Energy is mobilized to fight our enemy, or to flee from the attack. Long term cellular building and maintenance are deferred, and the immune response slows until after the threat has passed. Pain is blunted, cognition sharpened. But the body's reaction to stress is short-sighted, inefficient, and costly. If it suppresses long term building projects too long, our cells are not repaired. If it suppresses the immune function, our body will be unprotected from infection. In the face of repeated stressors, the body may be able to temporarily retain homeostasis, but the efforts to do so will eventually wear it down. The stress response itself will become harmful (Sapolsky, 1994).

Stress And Change

So what about the stress that comes with all the fun things in life like, going on vacation, graduating from college, getting married? Positive events that require us to change our daily patterns or rituals also cause stress. Selye defined the stress of positive events as "eustress" and the stress of negative events as "distress."

In landmark research, physicians Richard Rahe and Thomas Holmes surveyed over seven thousand people and analyzed the degree of change in their lives and the occurrence of any new illnesses. They developed a rating scale to predict illness based on the frequency and severity of life change (Holmes & Rahe, 1967). Common life changes are given a high or low score according to the proportionate degree of stress they elicit and the amount of readjustment required. Holmes and Rahe found that a score exceeding 300 in one year predicted an eighty percent probability of developing a serious illness. Forty-three events are included in the scale with a scores ranging from 100 down to 11. Death of a spouse and divorce are listed as the most stressful events. Illness (personal or family member), retirement and change in financial status score in the mid range. Vacation, Christmas season, a change in residence, church activities or work hours are at the lower range of stressful events.

I remember a stressful time in my life when, according to this scale I should have become sick. I'll explain this stressful time in terms of the Holmes-Rahe scale. My son Ken was two months-old (39 points) when my husband decided to leave our marriage (65 points). After a few months I moved 800 miles away (20 points), to live with my brother (24 points), and started a new job (29 points) to support myself and my son on a part time salary (38 points). Within another few months, I moved into my own house (24 points). Then my husband filed for divorce (73 points). I achieved a grand total of 312 points on the Readjustment Scale! Now, as I look back on that year filled with major changes, I think it's amazing that I didn't get sick. But that was also when I decided to go to Clown School. I believe it was the "humor therapy" that buffered my negative moods and protected my immune system from the stress of change.

Stress Management

Successful management of stress involves attaining a feeling of control, finding an outlet for frustration, and creating the perception that things can improve (optimism!). Everyone's attempt to cope with stress is unique, personal, and dependent on the interpretation of the severity of the threat.

Humor and laughter can be an antidote to stress. An ability to access humor during stress, when we feel angry, anxious, or embarrassed, will help us manage a tense experience. A sense of humor helps us take charge and create a positive emotion from what appears to be a negative event. This is important if we hope to gain some degree of control in a difficult situation.

Julie was an operating room nurse. During a relatively simple laparoscopy procedure (looking through a lighted tube into the abdomen) the equipment began to malfunction. The light at the end of the tube began to flicker on and off. The surgeon yelled "Fix the light." She quickly checked and rechecked all the connections and plugs, but it continued to flicker. The surgeon yelled louder. She rechecked everything again and found nothing broken. Finally, in exasperation, the surgeon yelled, "Doooooo Something!!!" Julie reached up and pulled a small container off of the anesthesia cart and began to shake it up and down, dancing and chanting like a Medicine Man during a healing ritual. Her action was so absurdly funny, that everyone laughed and the tension of the moment was released and everyone relaxed.

Stress Management Techniques:
- ♥ Write a memo congratulating yourself for being so wonderful.
- ♥ Answer a highly technical question in your best Donald Duck voice.
- ♥ Take an eight hour lunch break.
- ♥ For a quiet evening, play a blank cassette at full volume.
- ♥ Pretend that you're someone else.
- ♥ Eat gelatin with chopsticks.
- ♥ Pretend that you're still in control.
- ♥ Ring somebody's doorbell and run away.

—Donna Strickland, RN, MS

Psychoneuroimmunology

Psychoneuroimmunology is the word used to describe the study of the connection between the emotional experience, the neurological response, and the immune function. Research in psychoneuroimmunology proves that a merry heart is like good medicine! Before we are able to understand this research, it is important to have a rudimentary awareness of the structure and function of the immune system and how it communicates with the cognitive and emotional areas of the brain (Ader, 1991).

Department Of Defense - The Immune System

Our body has a highly refined system that protects us from invading and harmful organisms. The system is composed of two distinct mechanisms: cellular immunity and humoral immunity. The cellular component of the immune system is composed of millions of white blood cells called leukocytes. The humoral component, which is not so-named because of its relationship to our sense of humor, but rather, because it refers to the activities of antibodies or immunoglobulins and the role they serve in protecting us.

To fight disease and preserve health, the immune system must RECOGNIZE foreign organisms or cancer cells. It must REMEMBER the invaders it previously encountered and which defense strategy was effective. And finally, it must RESPOND appropriately to the invading substance. If the immune system under-reacts to threat because it fails to recognize or remember an invader, the result could be death from an overwhelming infection. If the body's own cells are rapidly reproducing out of control and are not recognized, the result could be cancer.

Mary's children recently broke out with chicken pox. Caring for them as a good mom, she was exposed to the virus. Her immune system RECOGNIZED the virus, REMEMBERED when she had chicken pox as a child, and RESPONDED by producing the appropriate sensitized cells and antibodies to kill the virus before it could begin to reproduce within her body.

The Infantry - Immune System

Like an army protecting the home land, the immune system protects the body from viruses, bacteria, fungi, and cancer cells. Specialized white blood cells called lymphocytes are manufactured in the bone marrow, (the porous inner spaces of the body's long bones) and are released throughout the body. Like soldiers leaving boot camp, many are shipped to other organs for specialized training (Sapolsky, 1994).

About half the lymphocytes, called T-cells, are trained in the thymus gland, a small organ behind the breast bone. These cells are especially important in organizing the immune response. As in any army, the cells maintain a specific rank and function. Some T-cells become "helper" T-cells that recognize invaders by their chemical aroma (chemotaxis). Others become "killer" T-cells serving as soldiers, armed and ready to attack. Some develop into "memory" T-cells, receiving information about successful attack methods and recalling this data upon demand in the future. Finally, there are the quality control cells called "suppressor" T-cells. Their job is to recognize when the battle is over and to recall the troops to their quarters for R and R! Another type of cell, called "phagocytes," are the vacuum cleaners who engulf and destroy foreign particles and debris after the messy battle.

Specialized lymphocytes called B-cells cluster near lymph nodes where they produce antibodies against potentially harmful microorganisms. These antibodies or immunoglobulins are released by B-cell lymphocytes when they receive a signal from the T-cells. Another specialized cell called the "natural killer" cell (NK) is highly trained to recognize and eliminate virus and cancer cells, without help from any other cells (Roitt et al., 1993; Kuby, 1994).

To function properly, the immune system must recognize and react appropriately to all invaders. Auto-immune diseases occur when the immune system mis-identifies a part of it's own body as an invader and mounts an attack.

Marie has rheumatoid arthritis. The joints of her fingers, shoulders, knees and ankles are swollen and extremely painful to move. Marie has an auto-immune disease. Her immune system is confused and unable to recognize that the tissues lining her joints actually belong in her body. The lymphocytes have launched an attack on these tissues, creating inflammation and swelling.

Allergic reactions occur when the immune system is hypersensitive to certain substances.

David has hay fever. Each spring, when the trees blossom and produce pollen, his immune system over reacts and mounts a full blown attack on the pollens, as if his life depended on it. His eyes begin to itch and water, he sneezes continually and he feels miserable, all because of an hypersensitive immune response.

An Imaginary Battle

Okay, now lets have some fun and take our army out for an imaginary battle. Let's say it is a bright, sunny day and you are walking barefoot in the park. Suddenly you step on a piece of dirty glass and cut your foot. Some of the dirt enters your blood stream where your immune cells are on constant patrol.

Immediately, your phagocytes (the vacuum cleaners) recognize the invading organisms in the dirt. They quickly gather and wrap themselves around the bacteria, engulf them, swallow them, and digest them. Because of their hasty gluttony, they burp, displaying little bits of the organism down the front of their nice clean uniforms. Now, please understand, they do not have bad manners. They are acting exactly as they are designed to. These phagocytes are called antigen-presenting cells, and that is precisely what they have done— they have presented the antigen (foreign protein) onto their uniforms!

Nearby, helper T-cells are able recognize this activity. How? Well, the surface membranes of all lymphocytes are covered with "satellite dishes," designed to receive messages. These are called receptor sites. The helper T-cells come close enough to touch their receptor sites to the surface of a phagocyte, and pick up the message of what the invader is composed of. Then they process this information and immediately send a fax to immune cells throughout the body. Wait a minute you say, a fax? Well, it's sort of like a fax, and is actually called a lymphokine, probably Interleukin 1. These lymphokines then travel through the blood stream and deliver messages to the killer T-cells who are then able to go to their arsenal and prepare the most effective weapon to kill the invaders! The killer T-cells also put out a call to arms throughout the immune system, and thousands of cells respond to the exact location of the invasion. The fax also arrives in the administrative offices of the B-cells, who then produce immunoglobulins (kind of like "smart bombs") that will aid the killer T-cell to attack and destroy the invaders.

All of this activity occurs within minutes to hours after your unfortunate encounter with the dirty glass chip, and may continue for days if the organism is strong and able to multiply quickly in the warm, protein rich environment of your blood and tissues.

Meanwhile, the quality control group, suppressor T-cells, watch carefully as the battle progresses. As soon as the invader has been overwhelmed, they blow the whistle for everyone to stop fighting and return to their normal patrol duties.

During the battle, the memory T-cell has been taking volumes of notes about which weapons and battle strategy was most effective. Then they enter this information into the database for quick retrieval, in case similar organisms enter the body in the future. As the battlefield clears, the phagocytes can be seen vacuuming up the remains of tissue and immune cells that were sacrificed during the war.

This is a very coordinated and highly specialized army that protects us from harm. The soldiers may be microscopic, yet they are as sophisticated as our modern armies. That is the good news; the bad news is that their performance can be rendered ineffective by our emotions, especially the emotions we experience during stress!

*Each human being possesses a beautiful system for
fighting disease. This system provides the body with
cancer-fighting cells—cells that can crush cancer cells or
poison them one by one with the body's own
chemotherapy. This system works better when the patient
is relatively free of depression, which is what a strong will
to live and a blazing determination can help to do.
When we add these inner resources to the resources
of medical science, we're reaching out for the best.*

—Norman Cousins

Immune Response to Stress

Scientists are studying how various degrees and duration of stress affect our immune systems at different stages of life, and how these changes might affect health and disease.

The Kiecolt-Glaser research team studied the immune response of medical students before, during and after exams (Kiecolt-Glaser, et al., 1986). They drew blood samples over a twenty-four hour period and found there was an increased release of stress hormones; and, a decrease in immune function, including a decrease in natural killer cells (NK). Many activities of everyday life involve pressures and anxiety, such as buying a house, paying taxes and work deadlines (No wonder they call it a "dead"-line!) Whether this decrease in immune function will actually lead to disease depends on how long the stress lasts, how you cope with it, and how healthy your immune system is.

Immunoglobulin A (IgA) found in our saliva, protects against upper respiratory infections such as colds and flu. Kathleen Dillon at Western New England College, measured salivary IgA levels before and after a humorous video, and found a significant increase in the concentration of salivary IgA after the video (Dillon & Minchoff, 1986). Remember that immunoglobulins or antibodies are produced by the B-cells, and offer specific protection against infections. This part of our immune system is very sensitive to moods. Research by Arthur Stone of SUNY, Stoneybrook found that salivary IgA levels were lower on days when the participants were in a negative mood and higher on days when they were in positive moods (Stone et al., 1987). Herbert Lefcourt in Ontario, Canada carried this one step further and found that subjects who tested higher for a more developed sense of humor showed a larger increase in salivary IgA concentration after viewing a humorous video (Lefcourt et al., 1990).

After a partner's death, the surviving spouse is at risk for infection. Grief is a profound emotion that is oftentimes overwhelming. Research shows that the loneliness and depression of a grieving spouse stimulates biochemical changes that weaken the immune system. Stephen Schleifer, of Mt. Sinai School of Medicine in New York, observed that recently widowed men showed a sharp drop in both the number and the activity of lymphocytes. This was first noted two months after the spouse's death, and up to ten months later (Schleifer, 1983). Similar findings have been reported by Bartrop (Bartrop, et al., 1977).

These and many other studies (Ader, 1991) have established that the brain and the immune system do communicate with each other. But how do they talk? Where do they connect? What language do they speak? The research in psychoneuroimmunology is attempting to define these connections by examining the emotional centers of the brain and the surface of the immune cells.

The Human Brain

The human brain is extraordinary, allowing us to appreciate art, music, and literature, as well as communicate with each other. However, the basic purpose of the human brain, like the brains of all animals, is to preserve health, well-being, and reproduce the species.

Millions of years ago, the structure of the brain was much more simple. As humans evolved new structures were added, but remnants of the older brain remained. The cerebral cortex, or thinking cap, developed about fifty million years ago and is responsible for sorting information coming from the senses, making decisions based on this information, and sending instructions to other parts of the brain and body.

Primitive parts of the brain are responsible for maintaining life and health. The oldest, and most primitive section of the brain (the brain stem) is responsible for breathing, heart rate, and the perceptions that are needed to find prey and avoid predators. Neuroscientist Paul MacLean, calls this section the "reptilian brain." Another portion of the brain developed to regulate emotion, body temperature, fluid and hormone balance (the mid brain). MacLean calls it the "early mammalian brain." Structures in this area include the hypothalamus and limbic system, centers for emotions and value processing. These areas are also a source of many chemical secretions (neuropeptides and neurotransmitters) that help regulate immunity (MacLean, 1985).

Obviously, there are connections between the older and younger portions of the brain. Stress from worries and troubling thoughts arise in the cerebral cortex, which then stimulates emotional responses in the limbic system which eventually effect our bodies through the secretions of neurotransmitters. Research is proving that emotions of optimism and joy, as well as depression and anger, influence our immune system.

The brain has a direct communication link to other parts of the immune system as well. David Felten identified nerve pathways between the hypothalamus and the spleen, lymph nodes and bone marrow, where most immune cells are produced (Felten et al., 1985). The brain talks to the immune system by sending messages directly through nerve pathways to organs of the immune system.

Neurobiologist Candace Pert is one of the most respected researchers in the area of mind-body medicine. As former Chief of Brain Biochemistry at the National Institute of Mental Health, she identified chemical messengers (neurotransmitters or neuropeptides) which are released from the brain during the experience of emotion. Pert wondered, if neuropeptides were linked to emotions, could they also be linked to immunity? Working with her husband, Immunologist Michael Ruff, they studied the influence of neuro-peptides on immune cells. Pert and Ruff discovered receptor sites on the surface of the immune cells. Once the neuropeptide attaches to the receptor site, the action of the immune cell frequently changes (Pert et al., 1985; Pert, 1986). These receptor sites are like television satellite receiving dishes that pick up signals sent from great distances. The limbic system of our brain broadcasts messages about our emotions by releasing neurotransmitters. These chemicals enter the blood stream and if they attach to the receptor site of a white blood cell, they can alter its behavior. Since we want to make immune cells work for our health, we should be sending happy emotional messages to them!

The road between the brain and the immune system is not a one way street. Immune cells are also able to communicate messages to the brain and other parts of the body. J.E. Blalock of the University of Alabama, discovered that white blood cells actually produce many of the same chemicals secreted by the brain (Blalock, 1983; Blalock 1989). The immune system is able to transmit, as well as receive information. Researchers are now beginning to think of the immune system as a sensory organ for the rest of the body, constantly sending information back to the brain about the status of immune cells, the presence of invaders and other important data.

In the last twenty years, we have moved from the belief that the immune system acts independent of the brain, to the knowledge that the immune system is influenced by the brain and now, to an entirely new possibility that the brain and the immune system may be working together for the body's health. This teamwork shows an integrated system that reflects both the importance of caring for our physical and emotional bodies, and most likely our spiritual body as well.

I am convinced that humor and laughter help us maintain an emotional balance during stress. They also enhance the function of the immune system, providing us with more protection from bacteria, virus and cancer. Humor

and laughter have therapeutic benefits and science offers proof that we
should 'Jest for our Health.' Science is finally embracing what some have
known for thousands of years:

*Let the surgeon take care to regulate the whole regimen of
the patient's life for joy and happiness, allowing his relatives
and special friends to cheer him.*

*—Henri de Mondeville, physician and
surgeon during Middle Ages*

CHAPTER CHAT

NANCY NURSE: Wow! I feel stressed out just reading all that scientific stuff! Is it really all that important?

NURSE KINDHEART: Well, dear, some people need to understand the graphs and statistics before they can believe that humor and laughter will improve their health.

NANCY NURSE: Yeah, yeah, but it seems obvious to me. If unpleasant emotions have a negative effect on our body, then pleasant emotions should have a positive effect, you know, make us feel good and healthy!

NURSE KINDHEART: Yes, dear. But health care professionals like to be more certain of findings and facts before they rush into anything new. They don't like surprises.

NANCY NURSE: Well, they should be happy with all the research studies and resources in this chapter!

NURSE KINDHEART: I'm sure they will be. Some of the caregivers are already aware of Holistic Health.

NANCY NURSE: You mean "Ho Ho Holistic Health!" We are talking about the connection between laughter and health here.

NURSE KINDHEART: That's cute, dear. Holistic Health like psychoneuroimmunology, connects and then treats the body, mind and spirit as one complete system. The body is the immune system. The mind is the neurological connection to the immune system. The spirit connects our emotions to the mind and eventually to the body's response.

NANCY NURSE: My, my, Nurse Kindheart! You're pretty smart for a clown!

Chapter 4
The Merry Heart:
Mirth Aide

*Over the years, I have encountered a surprising number of instances
in which, to all appearances, patients have laughed themselves
back to health, or at least have used their sense of humor
as a very positive and adaptive response to their illness.*

—Raymond Moody MD

Robert lay quietly in his hospital bed. The doctors had visited and left, the nurses were finished with their morning care. It was quiet, he was alone and feeling lonely. His wife, Sally, and the kids would not be able to visit until later that evening. What could he do until then? It was hard not to worry about his surgery scheduled for the next day. The more he worried, the more he felt agitated, depressed, and simply scared to death. In the next moment, he was given the perfect solution. Evelyn, a smiling volunteer entered his room pushing a funny little cart. She wore a colorful smock and a silly hat labeled, "Humor Patrol—Department of Energy." Robert smiled for the first time that day. "Looks like you could use some 'Mirth Aide,' and we've got a wonderful selection today."

Robert was skeptical, but curious. He asked for an explanation. "Well," she replied, "it's difficult for patients to lie around all day waiting for the next medical procedure. They worry a lot and then get depressed. These negative emotions have been proven to inhibit healing, so to prevent them, we provide a therapeutic humor program for our patients. It's part of the hospital's mission statement, to offer care and attention to the whole patient: body, mind and spirit."

Robert agreed his spirits needed a lift, and his mind could use some distraction. He asked to see more. First, Evelyn opened the "Yuk-a-Day Vitamin" jar and read a few jokes, riddles and funny one-liners. Then she opened a drawer and pulled out a few wind up toys and started running them around his overbed table. She continued to pull out toys, games, props, puppets, cartoon books, puzzles and costume items. Soon both of them were laughing, joking and playing around like small children. After performing a few magic tricks, Evelyn gave Robert a list of the humorous audio tapes, video programs and funny books that were available from the hospital's Laughter Library. Robert chose an audio tape of Bob Newhart, his favorite comedian and scheduled a comedy video to be delivered when his family arrived that evening. He selected a few toys to borrow, some rubber vomit to tease the nurses, and a squirt gun to defend himself against unwanted interruptions.

Robert felt like a kid again, filled with enthusiasm and ready to have fun. He looked forward to the fun and laughter he would experience and share with his family. As Evelyn was leaving, she offered one more answer to a problem he had not yet solved. "If you like, we can schedule a clown to visit with you while you're in the hospital." "Great idea," he thought. Robert Jr.'s birthday was on Saturday and instead of missing his party, now they could share a special celebration right there in the hospital. He scheduled the clown visit. Because of the therapeutic humor program, Robert was now feeling energized, optimistic and relaxed. Laughter *is* the best medicine!

What is a Therapeutic Humor Program?

The purpose of therapeutic humor programs is to bring laughter to patients, families, and staff. During moments of laughter, your attention is focused on enjoyment and amusement rather than on anxiety and pain. A humor program does not eliminate the cause of fear and frustration, but rather, it provides a momentary relief from the tension. Humor programs come in a variety of shapes and sizes. As with panty hose, it's not true that "One Size Fits All." You must combine elements from many different formats to create a program specifically tailored for your needs, limits and audience. People's preference for humor will vary dramatically, so to insure success, collect a wide variety of items. Some of the successful humor programs throughout the United States include things such as, Humor Rooms, Comedy Carts, Humor Baskets, Laughter Libraries, and, Clown Visits. This chapter will help you choose, plan and implement a program for your hospital, clinic, or home care setting.

Humor Rooms

A Humor Room is a place where patients, their families and staff can gather to share an opportunity to laugh, play and relax together. These rooms are decorated with comfortable furniture, plants, and art work. The furniture is arranged in clusters so that groups of three to five people can gather around a game table, television or reading area. The humor room at Baptist East Hospital in Louisville, Kentucky is called the "Oasis." Large ferns and palms surround the white wicker furniture to capture the mood of its name. In the corner, a player piano provides fun, uplifting music. Book shelves display humorous books, cartoon albums, board games, and stuffed toys. A hospital volunteer or student intern from the local seminary supervises the room and helps patients and families choose a humorous activity. They check out books and tapes from the "Laughter Library" and assist with the use of the VCR, audio tape players and games.

One of the first humor rooms, "The Lively Room," was created at DeKalb Hospital in Decatur, Georgia by Sandra Yates, RN and a hospital board member, W.W. Lively. It was established in the large, sunny atrium space on the oncology unit. This room served as both inspiration and prototype for many other programs around the US. (See the Appendix for a partial listing of other humor rooms). The humor room setting provides a place for informal patient support, structured group sessions, and even, on occasion, the site of celebrations, such as wedding anniversaries, birthdays, and the completion of chemotherapy (Buxman, 1991).

Humor rooms do have some limitations. The location site is permanent and limits access for patients from other areas of the hospitals. Seriously ill hospital patients are usually unable to leave their room because of pain, cumbersome equipment, or physician orders, so they are not able to benefit from a humor room. Because of this, many hospitals provide comedy carts or mobile programs to bring much needed humor relief to the bedside. The humor room is ideal for long term care facilities, rehabilitation programs, psychiatric units or outpatient clinics.

George had an appointment at the University Hospital Clinic. He usually had to wait for an hour or more before his team of doctors was ready to see him. By the time he was called for his appointment he was irritated, hypertensive and grumpy. In fact, he was so upset that he barely remembered the advice his doctors prescribed. His care was compromised. One day, after he checked in with the receptionist, he was told he could sit in the central waiting room, or he could step down the hall and wait in the new humor room. George chose the humor room, and found a selection of videotapes, cartoon books, and joke books. He selected an old favorite, a Candid Camera video. He settled back in the comfortable chair and began to laugh. What seemed like only moments later, he heard his name being called for his appointment. 'Gee, they're on time today, what a surprise,' he thought. A glance at his watch, however, confirmed that he had actually waited the usual 60 minutes, but this time he entered the examination room much more relaxed and feeling jovial!

Comedy Carts

A Comedy Cart is a mobile unit with many of the same supplies that a humor room has (except the player piano)! It can be wheeled into a patient's room to bring mirth-aide right along side the frightening medical equipment and monitoring devices. These carts have been called a "Laughmobile; Jokes on Spokes; Humor on a Roll; or, Humor ala Cart." Some of them are similar to the library carts we see in old prison movies. Remember "The Bird Man of Alcatraz?" Burt Lancaster's old friend would push a library cart to the inmate's cells and offer books and magazines.

Other carts look more like big red tool boxes on wheels, full of drawers and cabinets that can be locked. Many hospitals use this type of cart for the emergency drugs and equipment that is brought into a patient's room during a cardiac arrest. I suggest you design a cart that won't confuse the patient about your intended therapy when you wheel it into the room! Most facilities like to design a colorful and festive cart which is custom made to fit their specific needs. Hospital engineering departments can usually do this if they have the time and resources, but you can also ask your local RSVP (Retired Senior Volunteer Program) or high school shop class to donate their time and skills.

One of the first comedy carts was created by Leslie Gibson, a nurse at the Morton Plant Hospital in Clearwater, Florida. She has prepared a guidebook and video program to help other facilities prepare comedy carts. The program includes guidelines for establishing a budget; obtaining supplies; designing a functional cart; and, suggested routines to use with patients and families. This is one of the best programs available for developing a comedy cart (See Appendix).

One of the finest carts I have seen is at the Fox Chase Cancer Center near Philadelphia. In 1995, I interviewed Terry Bennet, RN for my column in the *Journal of Nursing Jocularity* and asked her to tell us about her cart. She explained, "We have a wide variety of videos and comedy audio tapes, which can be played on a portable tape player with headphones. We have many toys, like squirt guns, Mr. Potato Head, yo-yos, kaleidoscopes, bubbles, whoopee cushions, slinkies, backgammon, checkers, crossword puzzles and some playing cards. We also have some funny costume items like a hat with dreadlocks attached, clown wigs, funny hats, and rubber noses. We received a donation of a Polaroid camera with an unlimited supply of discounted film from a local camera shop. This is great, because we can capture joyful moments on film, which are often real treasures for the family."

One of Terry's most popular videos is by Joe Kogel, called "Life and Depth." He's a cancer survivor and does a very funny presentation about using humor to preserve your attitude and keep your hopes up (See Humor Resource List). This is a tape often enjoyed by patients with their whole family. They have a great selection of other popular videos including, "Big" with Tom Hanks, "Wayne's World" for adolescents, Laurel and Hardy, Charlie Chaplin and Buster Keaton films for the seniors, and, of course, Lucille Ball film (Wooten, 1995).

Terry said that they leave their cart in the hallway so people can see it. It's about six feet high with big clown faces as the cabinet door handles. The doors are glass, so that people can see what's inside. They keep it locked to prevent theft, and the key is kept with the nursing staff. If someone from another floor wants to borrow it, they have to sign it out and they are responsible for replacing any lost or broken items.

All of the items on the cart should be labeled with identification numbers for easy inventory and record keeping when they are used by patients. A small tape player with ear phones can be provided for personal use when the noise must be kept down. A color TV and VCR can be included on the cart or provided separately to the patient.

Ideally, a "humor volunteer" would push the cart from room to room, offering a brief but entertaining introduction of the items available to be checked out. Another option is to have a list of the comedy cart items in each room. The patient would make his selections and then place a phone order with the Therapeutic Humor Office. A volunteer would bring the desired item to the patient's room, and assist them with operating the equipment. Be sure voice mail will receive calls if the humor office is empty (Gibson, 1995).

We can see from Robert's story that a comedy cart is ideal for hospitalized patients. A home care setting does not need such an elaborate or mobile unit.

Humor programs in the home can be best served by creating a humor basket. A basket is an inexpensive way to gather comedy supplies and can easily be transported to wherever humor is needed!

Humor Baskets

A Humor Basket is a smaller collection of comedy materials often used by family caregivers to bring moments of laughter to their loved one at home. Hospital staff find that humor baskets stimulate their own creativity, enhances their spontaneity and provides quick access to items with humor potential. You may also be tempted to use these items for your own personal stress reduction program. A Humor Basket is an easy therapeutic humor program to create, and is an appropriate place to start if you have limited time or resources.

Cathy Johnson, RN, has created Humor Baskets for Dartmouth-Hitchcock Medical Center in Lyme, New Hampshire (Johnson, 1995). As a compassionate nurse, she was sensitive to her patients needs and recognized how bored and depressed they became during lengthy hospitalizations and prolonged bedrest. She didn't have generous funding for an extensive humor program, but she wouldn't let that stop her from providing her patients with the "comic relief" they needed.

Cathy used a large wicker basket and filled it with assorted toys and gadgets that caused silly giggles and were fun to play with. You may even include "joke jars" that look like medicine bottles and contain strips of paper with snappy one liners such as:

- ♥ You know you're getting older when you lean over to tie your shoes, and you ask yourself, what else can I do while I'm down here?
- ♥ I can't figure out which covers less, the hospital gown or my insurance company.
- ♥ Traffic was so bad on the freeway the other day, on the way home I had to stop three times to make car payments.

- ♥ My doctor is very conservative. If he doesn't need the money, he doesn't operate.
- ♥ Men are bachelors by choice. Sometimes it's their choice; sometimes the choice of the women they meet (Perret, 1992).

Gerontologist and humor specialist, Betty O'Malley, suggests putting jokes appropriate for different age and gender groups into different jars labeled, 'Child, Adult, Classic, Male or Female' (O'Malley, 1992b).

Kathleen is a nurse in the Intensive Care Unit of a large hospital. Her patients are frequently too sick to appreciate humorous interaction, but she realizes the importance of using humor to reduce her own stress level on the job. At the end of a particularly exhausting twelve-hour shift, filled with one crisis after another, a dedicated physician refused to leave a patient's bedside for fear that another crisis would arise in his absence. He had not had a meal for almost ten hours and complained about his unbearable hunger. He asked Kathleen to find him something to eat. She told him that the hospital kitchen was closed and all she could offer him was juice and custard from the patient's snack refrigerator.

He pouted, and said he had something more flavorful and substantial in mind. She agreed to search the other units, knowing that her search would be futile. Wanting to offer the physician some sort of relief, she went to the humor basket and found the rubber chicken. She tied a blue ribbon around its neck and folded it neatly on a tray and then covered it with an aluminum plate cover. She brought the tray to the physician and excitedly announced that her search was successful and he could now have a tasty meal. Eagerly, the physician lifted the plate cover, and the rubber chicken unfolded onto the tray. At first he didn't appreciate the joke, and impatiently asked, "Just what is this supposed to be?" Kathleen looked at the chicken with the blue ribbon and announced, "Well, that's Chicken Cord en Bleu." They both laughed and he gratefully consumed his juice and custard.

Collecting Humor Supplies

As you prepare your humor room, basket or comedy cart, finding funny props, toys, hats, and costume parts may present the greatest challenge. Fortunately, many mail order catalogs offer high quality, amusing supplies. To find some of the gadgets we've discussed, peruse the Humor Resource section at the end of this book. Some of the best sources I have found are, Clown Supply Catalog; Archie McPhee; Oriental Trading Company; Peechy Keene Props; Costumes by Betty; Anatomical Chart Company and, United Ad Label.

Supplies for Humor Programs

Joke Books	Wind Up Toys
Kaleidoscopes	Rubber Noses
Large Sunglasses	Goofy Hats
Cartoon Albums	Audio And Video Tapes
Giant Pacifier	Clown Nose
Puppets	Magic Wand
Rubber Chicken	Smile On A Stick
Foam Granite Rocks	Funny Pictures
Cartoon Books	Joke Medicine Bottles
Funny Post-It Notes	Groucho Glasses
Funny Buttons	Hand Held Games
Squirt Guns	Coloring Books And Crayons

Laughter Libraries

Most humor enthusiasts have a collection of funny books, audio and video tapes. I can hardly resist purchasing a book that makes me laugh, because I know there will be some days when I can't access my "comic vision" or see anything funny about a stressful situation. That's when I count on my humor collection to "see me through." Every home, every hospital unit, every business should have a collection of books and tapes available for times when "terminal seriousness" threatens to remove the joy from our lives.

Laughter libraries offer a selection of funny and informative books about humor and health. Audio and video tapes are usually a part of this collection. These resources can be used either at home or within a facility. There are literally hundreds of books that can be included in a laughter library. I have provided a list of some of my favorite books for humor programs in the Appendix. But, remember, as I have repeated over and over in this book, one person's humor is another person's ho-hum. You can order books and tapes sight unseen from catalogs, but they may not tickle your funny bone. I suggest that you scout the humor section of large bookstores at least once a month, to discover new and funny material. An even easier solution, is to subscribe to a humor newsletter that reviews new books and offers a sample of their contents. A list of some of the best newsletters and publications are provided in the Humor Resource section of this book.

Caring Clown Programs

Most of us are familiar with the circus or parade clown. We remember them as bold, bumbling, and boisterous. They enter the circus ring chasing each other, slipping and falling, sneaking up to startle other clowns and then running away. In contrast, the caring clown working in a hospital, nursing home, or on a home visit, is quiet, gentle, and empathetic. A good, caring clown is sensitive enough to read non-verbal body language, and has good listening skills. Bedside clowning attempts to distract patients from their problems to help them forget their pain. Patients are given a chance to watch or participate in some fun and silliness. Clowns offer a momentary release from personal burdens, inspire joy, and stimulate the will to live.

Clown visitation programs exist in hundreds of hospitals and home care organizations throughout the United States. Perhaps the most well-known is "Big Apple Circus - Clown Care Unit" in New York City. Under the creative guidance of founder and Director, Michael Christensen, it currently has 30 clowns who regularly visit New York hospitals (Darrach, 1990). The Clown Care Unit recently expanded their program to include the largest pediatric hospital in the United States, Boston Children's Hospital. In 1995, the Clown Care Unit received a $150,000 research grant from the Richard and Hilda Rosenthal Center for Complementary Medicine, to monitor the clown's visits in six metropolitan hospitals. The goal of this year-long study is to measure the therapeutic effect of the clown's visits. Since its inception in 1986, The Big Apple Clown Care Unit has been a wonderful model for many other Caring Clown programs around the country. A few of these programs are listed in the Appendix.

Richard Snowberg is an Associate Professor of Education at the University of Wisconsin at LaCrosse. He is also the Director of Clown Camp, a summertime series of week long, residential training programs. If you would like to learn the art of clowning, Clown Camp is a great place to start (See Humor Resource List). Richard assembles an impressive faculty of professional clowns from the United States and abroad. Students can choose from several specialty tracks, and one of the most popular is the Caring Clown track. They learn skills and routines appropriate for clowns in hospitals and nursing homes.

Richard's book, *The Caring Clowns,* is an inspiration and a guide for the clown that wants to develop bedside clowning skills. In his book he says, "In some instances, while dispersing therapeutic humor as a caring clown, or confronting individuals experiencing untold pain, you may never know what impact you've made on given individuals. . . Your influence and impact may be more strongly felt by those around the patients or residents, than by the patients themselves. Health care providers, such as nurses may be effected more than the patient. As a clown you may never know how you are perceived by those that see you. In fact, you may never know that some people have seen you, as they watch from afar" (page 17).

One of my favorite stories from Richard's book describes the work of Eloise Cole from Scottsdale, Arizona. She is probably the only clown in the country that is employed by a mortuary! (Grimshaw Mortuaries in Phoenix) Eloise is a bereavement specialist, who utilizes her clown character, Rainbow, to bring out the fears, questions, guilt and other emotions adults and children feel after experiencing a death. Her clown is by no means the only vehicle she uses in her work, but she believes that it adds to the power of her communication. She has developed a presentation she calls, "Rainbow the Clown and Her Balancing Act of Grief."

When Rainbow appears, she makes an entrance with a bouquet of helium-filled balloons to soft background music. She approaches the audience and slowly hands out the balloons, bonding with the mourners. Using a variety of props, she describes her feelings, while telling a story.

'I am a very happy clown, but at one point in my life I was very sad. I had a big frown and was really down.' I then relate that the love of my life was the light of my life—I use the magic light bulb trick—and then one day the light went out. I cried and cried and felt that my heart had turned upside down. I turn a heart on my costume, which adheres with Velcro, upside down. I use a "CLOSED" sign to demonstrate that my world seems to have closed down. I talk about feeling pain, that I carry it around all the time, and can't get rid of it. I use tangled wine colored yarn to represent pain.

I dust the audience with a feather duster, because if I keep busy enough, maybe I won't think about all that pain. I drag a clock on the floor because time drags. A cloth globe I carry on my shoulders symbolizes I am carrying the weight of the world on my shoulders. A small dumbbell is my symbol for telling myself I must be strong. My wilting flower demonstrates that my whole life seems different, that even the flowers in my garden are different.

I hold up a "NO TRESPASSING" sign because I do not want to be around my friends who are happy. I pull more pain (yarn) from my pocket and I seem to have pain coming out all over the place. I pick up two puppets who are my family and take care of them so that I will be distracted from my pain. I begin to feel really nuts, by shaking a can of nuts, and I may come uncorked, by showing a bottle with the cork askew and more pain coming out of it. I feel CRAZY.

I hold up my, "CAUTION: WATCH YOUR STEP!" sign. I know I need help. I take a "HELP WANTED" sign into the audience and ask for assistance. I take my puppets and ask people to help me care for my family. I have two giant ears and ask that two people listen to me, I need to talk about the changes in my life.

I remind myself to eat right and get plenty of rest using a small pillow. I likewise avoid alcohol and drugs with a large scoop. My heart turns around part way and I am beginning to feel better. A butterfly on a wand reminds me that if I am going to get better I will need to change, as my world has changed. I use a flashing foam star wand to remind me that I have new stars on my horizon and a string of colored hearts demonstrates that I can have new and different loves in my life. A large star wand in rainbow colors is my finale—the magic and wonder of the rainbow really lies within you and me and sometimes we need to rebuild our own rainbows (Snowberg, 1992, pp. 109-111).

Rainbow's program takes about twelve minutes. Following her presentation, Eloise talks about grief or conducts a support group. She currently conducts about 15 programs a month, about one quarter of them as Rainbow. Eloise admits she was scared when she began the program because grief is not funny, and clowning is not an established medium for talking about grief. Rainbow's success as a caring clown for a very special group affirms that people can and do respond to heartfelt humor as a way to cope with life's difficulties.

Caring Clown Guidelines and Routines That Work

While a stage clown measures success by audience laughter or applause, the caring clown's reward is a smile, a tender "thank you," or tears. If you are a clown establishing a new relationship with a hospital or nursing home, you should first go to the facility in street clothes and meet with the appropriate staff (Child Development Specialist or Nursing Supervisor) to obtain permission and establish guidelines. Many hospitals may not have guidelines regarding entertainers who visit patients, so have some information and guidelines to offer. Convince them of your professionalism and your intent to work with the system to develop a program that will benefit both the hospital and the patients.

If you are developing guidelines for a Clown Visitation program at your facility, advise your prospective clowns:

- ♥ Look sharp and clean; even if you are a hobo clown.
- ♥ Costumes should communicate fun and fantasy and not be threatening in any way.
- ♥ Bedside audiences should be kept small (one to three people).
- ♥ Individualize your performance according to who is present.
- ♥ Plan your routines so that they do not depend on the patient's verbal or physical response—perform so that the patient may simply observe you and be entertained.

Suggested Guidelines for Clown Visitation Programs

- ♥ All visits will be pre-approved and scheduled prior to arrival.
- ♥ Clown visits occur between 9 AM and 8 PM and will avoid all meal times.
- ♥ Clowns will check in at the nursing station, obtain feedback and suggestions for patient visits, and request the staff to accompany him/her to the patient's room on the first visit.
- ♥ Clowns will ask (from the doorway) for each patient's permission before entering their room.
- ♥ Clowns will not move any patient or manipulate hospital equipment—the staff will be called if necessary.
- ♥ Clowns will not wear gloves, unless instructed to by the staff. They will wash their hands prior to exiting the room.
- ♥ All gifts will be approved by the nursing staff before being given to a patient.
- ♥ Visits will be limited to ten minutes, unless the staff permits longer visits.
- ♥ After visits are complete, clowns will check in at nursing station to obtain other requests or notify them that they are leaving the facility.

Routines that Work

I have interviewed several caring clowns to gather ideas and suggestions that may help anyone interested in learning bedside clowning skills. Richard Snowberg and Kenny Ahern from Clowns on Call in LaCrosse, Wisconsin; Bonnie Donaldson from St. James Hospital in Chicago Heights, Illinois; and, Janet Tucker from Hammond, Indiana, have offered the following tips for those interested in developing a caring clown routine:

Announce your arrival and get permission from the patient to enter the room.
- ♥ Read their expressions and non-verbal gestures to determine if you are welcome.
- ♥ Blow bubbles into the room before entering.
- ♥ Sound a bird-whistle and then insert a clown shoe inside the door.
- ♥ Toss a silk scarf into the room and pull it back, each time working your way a little further into the room.
- ♥ Ask your hand puppet, "Do you think it's okay for us to come in here?" After the puppet nods, ask the patient if it is okay.

Work with a partner.
- ♥ Opening remarks and antics can be made between the clowns while the patient observes and becomes more comfortable.
- ♥ Enter the room and begin to discuss the plans for the "big party" to be held in the patients' room later in the day. Notice that the flowers have arrived, ask the patient if he has ordered the band and ice cream yet.
- ♥ Announce that everyone who's been in the hospital more than one hour is entitled to a free haircut and pull out giant scissors and a comb, as your partner fervently tries to talk the patient out of accepting the offer.
- ♥ Enter the room and announce to the patient that you will be giving them a parking ticket because they've been in the hospital too long.
- ♥ As you develop and change your routine and props, simply ask the patient, "Would you like to see something that might help you feel better?"

<u>Props communicate</u> the comedy and absurdity.
- ♥ Show a large plastic bone labeled, "Funny Bone" and ask if the patient has lost his funny bone recently.
- ♥ Use a stethoscope to listen to toes, ears and knees.
- ♥ Offer a 'three piece chicken dinner' and then display three kernels of corn.

<u>Leave a small gift</u> with the patient to remind them of your visit.
- ♥ Paper puzzle sheet with games, riddles, and puzzles to solve.
- ♥ Cartoon caricature of a clown for the patient to color.
- ♥ Clown dollar to help with hospital expenses.
- ♥ Colorful playful stickers to apply to the water pitcher or hospital gown.
- ♥ Polaroid camera photo taken of the clown and patient.
- ♥ Avoid gifts of food, (unless approved by hospital staff); balloon animal sculptures (which may cause suffocation) or any sharp object (which might be harmful).

As you continue to clown, add successful routines to your list and drop the ones that don't' get a laugh. Read humor newsletters and books to develop funny routines. Remember to keep your heart open and let your love shine through your eyes! Stay in touch with your laughing spirit, for it is the spirit in the laughter that heals and comforts.

Hospital Clown Newsletters

"The Heart-to-Heart Caring Clowns" organization in Oakland, California publishes a quarterly Hospital Clown Newsletter. It is written by Shobhana Schwebke, "ShobiDobi," a clown who performs regularly for patients at Oakland's Kaiser Permanente Hospital. This eight-page newsletter is filled with practical ideas as well as suggested readings. It features proven routines to use during "clown rounds."

The newsletter has provided me with some great riddles:

> Q: What is the difference between a hill and a pill?
> A: A hill is hard to get up, a pill is hard to get down!

> Q: What kind of mistake does a ghost make?
> A: A Boo-Boo!

> Q: How do you keep from getting a sharp
>   pain in your eye when you drink chocolate milk?
> A: Take the spoon out of the glass!

Dr. ShobiDobi provides great prop ideas and suggestions for funny routines. For example, she created a stethoscope with a tiny tea cup at one end and big red sponge balls at the ear ends. Not only is this visually amusing, but she uses it to listen to the child's toes or knees. Inside her vest she has attached many funny and silly sound devices that she has removed from old talking story-books. After listening the to heartbeats of staff and family members, she asks permission to check the patient's heart. Kids love to hear their heart snore or chirp! She listens carefully, discovering a giggle in their heart. She then places a smiley-faced sticker on the patient's wristband (being careful not to cover any vital information) and informs the patient that, "This is to warn the doctor that there's a giggle in your heart!" (see Humor Resource List for more information).

LaughMakers magazine also features articles and interviews with successful Caring Clowns. They provide guidelines and resources to build your hospital clown program and improve your "bedside manners" (See Humor Resource List).

A Clown's Story

Karen McCarthy, aka, "Poop Deck" the clown, relates one of her most touching clown experiences in a letter to the American Association for Therapeutic Humor. She explains, "I was in costume at Sloan-Kettering Cancer Center when I was asked to visit Justin, a seven year-old boy with multiple cancerous tumors, including one that would necessitate amputation of one of his legs. I stepped into the room and Justin's intelligent eyes were wild like a caged animal. "Operation Desert Storm," he said. "They're gonna take my leg." "That's what I hear," I said, almost unable to cope with his directness. "I'm not going to be able to stop them am I?" I shook my head no.

From that point on we decided to make the best of it. I asked him what he wanted to do. He said he wanted to jump up and down on the bed. I said I'd squirt anybody that tried to stop him. We talked about how it can be scary coming out of surgery when you don't know where you are. So I told him to choose one thing out of my bag that I would have put on his bed after surgery so he would know he was okay. Justin picked my "Happy Crab" because, he said, "Even though it's a sad thing I have to do, it's a happy thing too."

The stretcher was wheeled in the room. Justin's eyes grew wild again. His mom and dad asked if I could go down to the OR with them. I gave Justin my squirt gun and said, "Only if Justin can cover for me." He squirted people all the way down. I think this experience is one of the most real things I have ever been through in my life. I will be forever grateful that I could be there for Justin and be a witness to his courage."

General Guidelines for All Types of Humor Programs

Leslie Gibson has prepared some guidelines for anyone interested in organizing a humor therapy program in their hospital, clinic or home (Gibson, 1995). Here are some tips to get you going:

- ♥ Prepare a list of appropriate audio and video tapes.
- ♥ Prepare a list of humorous books.
- ♥ Prepare a list of toys and games that can be used in bed.
- ♥ Collect cartoons and create an album.
- ♥ Collect costumes items.
- ♥ Collect gags and props appropriate for bedside humor.

- ♥ Establish a humor bulletin board in the hallway of patient units.
- ♥ Be sure to offer a wide variety that are suitable for all ages.
- ♥ Keep a log book for checking materials in and out.
- ♥ Provide a locked box on the cart for easy return of books and videos.
- ♥ Begin a humor program with a small target area, preferably with long term patients.
- ♥ Plan a big party to introduce your program to the hospital and community. Have clowns, balloons, and musical entertainment.
- ♥ Keep the Comedy Cart visible on the floors to stimulate interest.
- ♥ Deliver and pick up patient requested materials.
- ♥ Encourage colleagues and family members to bring in cartoons.
- ♥ Distribute sheets of riddles and encourage patients to share them with their caregivers and families.
- ♥ Be cheerful, smile, and have a good time!
- ♥ Scan your local TV program schedule and create a list of humorous entertainment options. Post this list in a common area.
- ♥ When using closed circuit video programs, be sure to obtain permission for use if it is copyrighted material. In some situations, you may have to purchase a license to show these films to large audiences.
- ♥ Encourage involvement of your staff through the hospital newsletter.
- ♥ Plan social events to bring attention to the humor program and reward volunteers.
- ♥ Ask patients to share their favorite humor items, and post a list of the most popular ones.

Humor Committee

The best way to insure the success of a Therapeutic Humor Program is to form a "humor advisory" committee and assign key people to work together in groups to create and implement your program. This committee might include staff from volunteer programs, the hospital auxiliary, pastoral care, social services, administration, and nursing. It would be good to include a representative from Home Health Care so that these services will be provided to the homebound and their family members. Any staff member with an interest and enthusiasm for humor should be welcome on this committee.

Nominate as Humor Coordinator, a person who is knowledgeable about therapeutic humor programs and is enthusiastic about the project. Tasks are assigned to members once the program is implemented, and the results are reviewed and evaluated by the entire committee. The committee tasks include writing a mission statement; developing the goals and objectives of the program; formulating and presenting a budget; developing policies and procedures; educating and informing staff about the therapeutic benefits of humor; obtaining supplies; securing ongoing financial support for the project from community resources, such as the Rotary, Lions, Elks, Kiwanis, and Junior League; and, every other task you can imagine!

The humor committee should meet every 4-6 weeks to update, brainstorm, and gather input from the staff who have seen the results of the program. Don't forget: these meetings should be fun and filled with the opportunity for laughter! The committee reviews supplies, videos and books for their appropriateness, safety, and "funniness factor." They are also responsible for assessing the value of the humor program by utilizing patient, family and staff surveys. This feedback should be used to improve the quality of humor service. You might reward those who complete a survey by inviting them to select a fun item, such as clown noses, funny Post-It notes, Groucho glasses, and funny buttons, from a special gift basket.

Patient Assessment of the Humor Program

Did the humor program make your stay with us more enjoyable?

Did the selection of tapes, books and materials have enough variety to suit your personal taste?

Rate the categories of videos, books, games, cassettes on a scale from 1 to 10.

We welcome your comments and suggestions.

CHAPTER CHAT - THE NURSES REPORT

NANCY NURSE: Wow, these comedy carts, humor rooms and laughter libraries are my kind of nursing!

NURSE KINDHEART: Well dear, if "A merry heart doeth good like a medicine," as the Bible says, then we should certainly see therapeutic humor programs among the available choices for medical treatment.

NANCY NURSE: I remember back in nursing school, the teachers used to nag to us with, "Stop fooling around, get serious, you'll have to get a job and earn a living some day."

NURSE KINDHEART: Isn't it delightful that now we can get paid for, as you say, "fooling around?" And, depending on what the patient needs, we can change from the ridiculous to the sublime.

NANCY NURSE: Yeah! Of course, I prefer the ridiculous and you prefer the sublime.

NURSE KINDHEART: Yes, and with the Caring Clown program, we will both have even more job security!

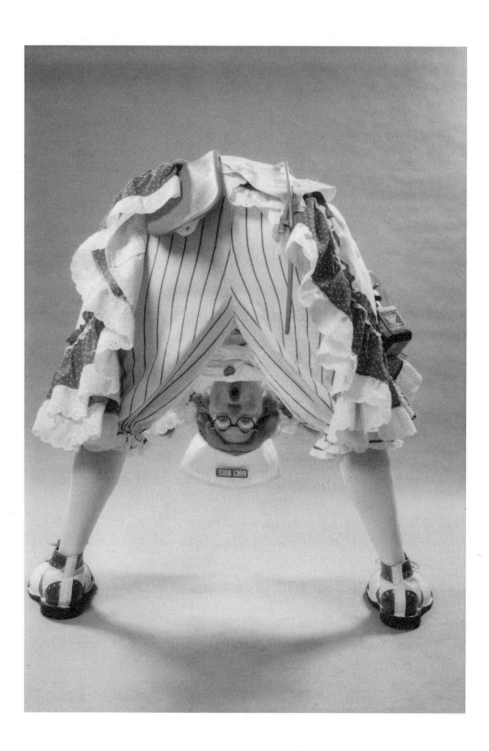

Chapter 5
The Foolish Heart:
Send in the Clowns

The art of the clown is more profound than we think. ...
It is the comic mirror of tragedy and the tragic mirror of comedy.
—Andre Suares

Let's begin with a story from a modern day clown as he begins his healing work. Wavy Gravy is an eccentric, outspoken political activist from Berkeley, California. He is also a deeply sensitive and compassionate clown. In his book, *Something Good for a Change,* he shares many of his adventures and humorous insights about life and living. One of my favorite stories about his clown work was presented in Ram Dass' book, *How Can I Help?* In this story, we see through his clown's eyes and feel through his clown's heart, what occurs when comedy is brought into tragedy.

"My idea was pretty simple at the beginning. I started to volunteer in wards with terminally ill children or burn victims, I'd just go in there to cheer them up a little, spread around some giggles. . . . It's a little tricky coming in. When some kids see a clown, they think they're going to be eaten alive. So it's always good to lead with some bubbles—just blow some bubbles around the ward. Then I move from bed to bed, just feeling out what's appropriate, maybe checkers, or blackjack, or go-fish. Or if they're lying there with tubes coming out of them, I'll hit the kids with riddles. Riddles are great.

The kids were very tough for me at the beginning—very. You see some pretty terrible things in these wards. Seeing children dying or mutilated is not something most of us ever get prepared for. Nobody teaches us to face suffering in this society. We never talk about it until we get hit in the face.

I was making the rounds one day at a children's hospital. I peeked into one room with badly burned children. There was this one little black kid in a bed. He was horribly burned. He looked like burnt toast. Pieces of his face weren't there. Pieces of his ears were missing. Where was his mouth? You could hardly tell who he was. There was no way of pinning a person to the face, what little there was left of it.

It was terrible, mind-boggling. My jaw dropped, I gasped, and I came completely unglued. I was overwhelmed. And my mind went off in all sorts of directions. So there we were, burnt toast and unglued clown. Quite a sight, I bet. And I'm fighting just to stay there, trying to find a way to get past my horror.

All of a sudden, this other little kid comes whizzing by—I think he was skating along with his IV pole—and he stops, and kinda pushes around me, and looks into the crib at this other kid, and comes out with, "Hey, YOU UGLY!" Just like that. And the burnt kid made this gurgling laugh kind of noise and his face moved around, and all of a sudden I just went for his eyes, and we locked up right there, and everything else just dissolved. It was like going through a tunnel right to his heart. And all the burnt flesh disappeared, and I saw him from another place. We settled right in.

Being able to look 'YOU UGLY,' in the eye . . that's done a lot for me. Because once I do that, I can go on to see what might be done that can ease things up. And you get all kinds of inspiration" (Dass, 1991, pp. 51-53).

Wavy Gravy is a healer. He uses comic qualities in an artistic way to bring joy and laughter to the serious, sometimes tragic moments of illness. Through outrageous antics, colorful costumes, and ridiculous props, he strolls into our hearts and heals with his wacky ways. He embodies many wonderful elements of the fool, the clown and the jester.

Fools, clowns and jesters have been a part of the healing arts for thousands of years. They bring "comic relief" into moments of tragedy and help us regain our balance. In our amusement, we are drained of our fears and worries and we are refilled with joy and delight! And these joyful, positive emotions stimulate our body's natural healing ability. This Chapter introduces you to the archetypes of the fool, the clown, and the jester, and traces their history through different cultures.

Bring on the Fools, Clowns, & Jesters!

These "laugh-makers" are seen in every culture. With their innocence, wit and antics, they help us to see reality in a different way. They reveal human nature in all its extreme of wisdom and foolishness. With their questions, stories, and absurd behavior, they challenge us to examine our beliefs, our abilities, and our sanity. These "delight-makers" ask us if our seriousness is really necessary and appropriate? With their comical routines, they laugh at our ridiculous ways and at the same time, show compassion for our suffering.

The Trickster

The trickster is a comical, mythological character of folklore and is seen in different cultures with both animal and human names. 'Coyote' is a familiar trickster in North American native cultures. The clever 'monkey' in Japanese stories is continually outsmarting and surprising the farmers. The sly 'fox' of European folklore gets into mischief and makes the audience wait for a magical moment.

In modern times, the trickster spirit is captured through characters such as Bre'r Rabbit, Tom Sawyer, Road Runner, and the infamous, Bugs Bunny. The trickster, possessing both intelligence and persistence, represents life in terms of a game: that tricking and being tricked are inevitable, but the reward for winning is that life may be experienced as an amazing and humorous surprise (Radin, 1972; Nisker, 1990; Hyers, 1996).

Bre'r Rabbit tricked Bre'r Fox into throwing him into the briar patch where he would be safe. Tom Sawyer tricked the other children into paying him for the "privilege" of white washing the fence, a chore Tom abhorred. Road Runner tricks Wiley Coyote into standing beneath the boulder which then falls and crushes him. Bugs Bunny tricks Elmer Fudd into looking down the barrel of his own shotgun, only to have it explode in his face! We all laugh at these antics as we observe from afar.

Coyote is a clever rascal who is sometimes given the role of creator in Native American mythology. One story tells of how Coyote has a sack full of stars that he is supposed to place in the sky. At first, he does a good job, placing the stars in neat rows, but soon he gets bored and restless. He finally tosses all the remaining stars into the sky, scattering them everywhere.

For hundreds of years, Coyote tales have been told by the elders of Native American tribes to instruct and entertain the community. These tales show how Coyote combines astute cleverness with perfect ignorance to create wildly comical situations. In the anthology, *Coyote's Journal,* Lowell Jaeger answers the burning question, "Why Dogs Smell Each Other's Butts."

> "When he asked to join in the sweat bath, the dogs refused him. 'You are unclean,' they told Coyote, 'you are not a dog.' So the dogs undressed for their bath and entered the sweat lodge without him. Coyote envied the glossy fur coats the dogs had hung outside the lodge. He thought of stealing them, but he decided not to. Instead he threw the long coats in a great pile, and wiped his muddy feet across them. Then he set fire to the sweat lodge roof and said in a loud voice, "Oh what will the dogs do now, Coyote has taken their fur!" From behind a rock, Coyote sat laughing as the naked dogs rushed into the cold out-of-doors, grabbing for a coat, afraid there might be too few to cover everyone. Years later, as the story goes, with every dog zipped into someone else's fur, dogs smell each other's butts, looking for their own. Meanwhile, Coyote is still grinning off in the hills some-where, rolling in red dirt, thinking how crude it is to be a dog, how much more clean, how much more fun to be Coyote!" (Jaeger, 1982).

Wes Nisker, in his book, *Crazy Wisdom,* captures the essence of coyote, "Coyote is most often seen with his head back, muzzle facing upward, howling at the moon. The secret of his crazy wisdom can be understood by listening closely to his cry. In it one can hear a bittersweet mixture of all experience. In Coyote's howl, we hear both longing and laughter, mocking and moaning" (Nisker, 1990, p. 29).

The Fool

Fools display simple mindedness for a comic effect. They represent a spirit and a perspective that stands apart from the laws of logic and society. Fools can be divided into two groups, the 'foolish fool' and the 'great fool.' The foolish fool is clumsy, inept and unsophisticated. Jerry Lewis is a good example of the foolish fool. The great fool is wise beyond ordinary under-standing. He doesn't try to fit in with society, but lives by his own rules. Wavy Gravy is a great fool. The foolish fool gets lost, the great fool is at home everywhere (Erasmus, 1941; Sexson, 1979; Nisker, 1990; Hyers, 1996).

Innocence is the trademark of the fool. The Fool lacks common sense and operates blissfully outside the laws of logic. In the movie, *King of Hearts,* a small French village is abandoned by its citizens to avoid confrontation by the invading Germans. Inadvertently, the locked gate of the insane asylum is left open and the patients escape, return to the town, and resume their former jobs. The barber has such a wonderful time cutting a man's hair that he pays his customer. The bishop delights in the array of sacramental robes and enthusiastically wears several of them in unusual combinations. The circus attendant feels sorry for the caged animals and releases all of them, petting each of them as they go free.

In the Arabic world, one of the most famous fools is Mulla Nasrudin. The Muslim mystics use stories about Nasrudin as spiritual lessons, giving him the role of either the village idiot or eccentric sage, capturing the essence of both the foolish fool and the great fool. Nasrudin is a short, stout man with an oversized turban on his head.

In one story, Nasrudin loses his precious donkey. He was panicked. His donkey carried his wares to the marketplace, provided comfortable transportation, and was his best friend. Nasrudin looked frantically all over town without success. Finally, he sat down with his friend to lament his terrible loss. He suddenly stopped his crying and announced, "Praise be to God that I was not on the donkey's back when he disappeared, for if I had been, we would both be lost!" Through this foolish and illogical perspective, he suddenly sees the blessings within his tragedy. This story gently invites the listener to apply this same crazy wisdom to their own predicaments to discover their hidden blessings (Leeming, 1979; Kornfield & Feldman, 1991; Hyers, 1996).

A story from the Hasidic Jewish tradition shows how the wisdom of a great fool can resolve a difficult situation. A rabbi was visited by a very poor man who complained of the crowded conditions of his home. He lived in a tiny one-room house with his wife, six children and mother-in-law. The rabbi inquired if the man had any animals. "Oh yes, I have chickens and a goat." The rabbi told the man to bring the goat inside to live with him. After a week, the man returned to the rabbi complaining that the situation was even worse than before, asking for more advice. The rabbi instructed the man to return home and bring the chickens into the house to live with him. The man objected, but did as he was told. A week later he came back to the rabbi, protesting that now his situation was worse than ever and he was going crazy. The rabbi told him to return home and take the goat and chickens out of the house. A few day later, the man came back smiling and grateful, saying, "Rabbi, my house is now so spacious and peaceful! You are certainly the wisest man who ever lived!" (Nisker, 1990, p.33).

Several years ago, I was going though some difficult times. My hospital had "down-sized" and my position was cut to part-time. Money was tight and I was worried and depressed. My friend Jane suggested we go for a bike ride to take my mind off my worries. My bike was lightweight and modern and Jane's bike was heavy and cumbersome. About half way through the ride, I suggested that we switch bikes. After some reluctance, she agreed and we continued the ride. My bike had small metal toe cages on the peddles so that after you inserted your foot, it was stable and couldn't slip off the peddle. Her bike had the standard flat peddles. As we peddled back into town, Jane was about a block ahead and I saw her riding toward a flower stand on the corner. Buckets of flowers covered the cart and surrounded it on the ground, and the attendant was sitting in a chair reading. She looked up as Jane approached. Jane slowed and finally stopped her bike right next to the flowers, forgetting that her feet were captured in the toe cages. She was unable to remove her foot in time to catch her balance. Jane and her bike tipped sideways and fell on top of the display, spilling water and crushing flowers. As she laid there, flailing about, shouting out apologies, the attendant sat with her mouth open in shock. Seeing the two of them in that ridiculous situation, I began to howl with laughter. I laughed until I cried, and couldn't stop laughing. And with the laughter, I released the tension, depression and worry that weighted my spirit and I felt cleansed and refreshed. And, I had a lot of slightly damaged flowers brightening my home!

Court Fools And Jesters

The position of the court fool has been discussed in history books as far back as the ancient Egyptian pharaohs. Most of us are more familiar with the court fools of the Middle Ages, known as jesters. These jesters were clever performers, delighting aristocratic audiences with their insight and biting wit. Though they were employed to make kings laugh by their foolish pranks, the jester also had considerable political and social power. With wit and humor, he ridiculed and criticized the king, but his observations were accepted because he made them funny. Courageous court jesters succeeded in bringing a spirit of free speech and healthy criticism to the royal court at a time when there were few viable checks on the monarch's power.

Court Fools helped kings to laugh at themselves which kept them in touch with their humanness. When Marot, a sixteenth-century jester walked alongside the king, the sovereign told him he could not bear having a fool on his right-hand side. "Is that so?" replied Marot, as he moved to the left of the king, "I can bear it very well." If the king identified with the jester, for that moment he came out from behind the facade of his serious self and gained a new perspective that was more human, flexible and compassionate (Towsen, 1976).

The Jester's costume evolved over many years. Early Roman Jesters shaved their heads except for a tuft of hair on top. The tuft was left to resemble a rooster's coxcomb, which was a symbol of foolishness. While the rooster or cock was considered a rather stupid bird, it still strutted about the barnyard, proudly crowing with a sense of authority. Today's Jester's hat actually evolved from more primitive hats that were made from the ears of jackasses, to which bells were added. As a Jester would make his silly and noisy appearance, the bells would announce his presence, and the merriment and revelry would begin.

The Jester carried a bauble, or a stick carved with a likeness of the Jester's head. He would have loud and ridiculous conversations with this comical character at the end of the stick, arguing and debating so that all could hear. Sometimes the carved image would seem to lean over and whisper an observation into the Jester's ear, which the Jester would then innocently announce to the king and his court. One story tells of a monarch who looked into a mirror and beheld his own aging face. New wrinkles had appeared and he began to wail at the sight. The court jester then listened to a message from the character on his bauble and began wailing and sobbing even louder. After the king regained his composure he asked the jester why he was carrying on so. The jester sobbed, "You weep over just one glimpse of yourself, but we have to look at you all day!" (Hyers, 1996, pp. 112-113).

Modern day court jesters hold politicians up to their own mirrors. These jesters include satirists like the "Capitol Steps," a musical group from Washington DC; cartoonist Gary Trudeau, the creator of Doonsbury; and, stand up comedians such as George Carlin.

The arrival of a good clown exercises a more beneficial influence upon the health of a town than of twenty asses laden with drugs.

—Sydenham

Historically, the appreciation of folly has thrived during difficult times of transition and change. Since ancient times, fools, clowns, and jesters have staged comical performances that topple traditional values and reverse political hierarchies, providing a healing balm for social concerns.

Church Fools

The fool provided a necessary mocking relationship in the spiritual as well as political kingdoms. The Feast of Fools in the Catholic church, was first seen in 12th century France. Despite harsh criticism from several Popes, it persisted until the Protestant Reformation in the 16th century. Religion and worship during the middle ages was serious, severe and highly controlled. There was little observable joy and celebration. Yet the human spirit needs joy to survive and thrive. The Feast of Fools is what anthropologist Max Gluckman called, "a ritual of rebellion." Because this rebellion was done in a comical way, it allowed conflicts and antagonisms to be played out without destruction to order and authority. The human spirit declares its strength and freedom, and reclaims a moment of joy (Nisker, 1990; Hyers, 1996).

You have everything, but one thing—Madness.
A man needs a little madness, otherwise, he never
dares to cut the rope and be truly free.

—Zorba the Greek

During the Feast of Fools, minor clergy of the church were allowed to usurp the roles of their superiors and engage in outrageous and blasphemous activities. These clergy would wear their sacramental robes inside out, hold their prayer books upside-down, sing wanton songs, dress up as women, and burn stinking incense made from the soles of their shoes. This "sanctioned rebellion" allowed the common people to vent their frustration and hostility at the powerful clergy and at the rigidity of religious doctrine. These foolish antics may seem arrogant and blasphemous, but theologian and humor scholar, Conrad Hyers explains, "True blasphemy is to be found not in humor as such, but in the absence of humor, for at the heart of the comic spirit and perspective is an acceptance of the prophetic warning against idolatry, and against that greatest blasphemy of all, the claim to understand or be as God" (Hyers, 1996, p. 120).

Religion can lift our spirit with visions of harmony and compassion, but it can also be a source of pride and segregation. Many of us have belonged to churches where some people exude a "holier than thou" attitude. By placing comic antics alongside pious acts, we are reminded of our humanity and foolishness.

In 1978, I belonged to a clown group in the San Francisco Bay Area. We offered our services to community organizations and churches. One minister of a local church asked a few of us to perform at a service he was holding on April Fool's Day. His sermon was about the importance of laughing at our own foolishness to maintain humility. As my character Scruffy, a tramp clown, I was in charge of sweeping the church floor as the worshipers arrived. My partner came tap dancing down the aisle singing, "Keep Your Sunny Side Up" and tossing confetti.

The funniest part of the whole program came in the middle of the preacher's sermon. Normally, he avoided the formal robes most ministers wore during services and instead sported a simple suit. That day, however, he wore the long black robe, clerical collar and a purple satin vestment. I'm sure the congregation was curious. He reached a point in his "humility" sermon where he told his listeners that he had not been completely honest with them about who he really was and what he really believed. The entire congregation leaned forward and you could hear a pin drop in the silence.

The preacher stepped out from behind the pulpit, took off his horn rimmed glasses and announced, "I believe in truth, justice, and the American way!" He threw open his robe and slung it over his shoulders like a cape. Underneath, he was wearing blue tights, red swimming trunks and a Superman T-shirt. He ran down the center aisle, around the church a few times and out the back door.

Everyone laughed uproariously—well, almost everyone—a few people shook their heads in disbelief wondering if they'd come to the wrong church. The minister had made his point: if you wish to remain humble, you can't take yourself too seriously, even if your expected role in life is to be serious.

Holy hilarity is alive and well today. The Fellowship of Merry Christians (FMC) is an organization of both clergy and lay people dedicated to bringing more joy and laughter into Christian worship and practice. FMC leader, Cal Samra, has written a wonderful book called, *The Joyful Christ,* in which he gives scriptural references to the importance of humor and Christian faith (Samra, 1986). FMC also has an excellent monthly newsletter filled with cartoons, jokes, amusing pulpit bloopers, and funny stories about kids in Sunday School. The Fellowship of Merry Christians' catalog has a large selection of books and tapes about Christian related humor (See Humor Resource List).

In Cedar Rapids, Iowa, St. Luke's Hospital has a Clown Ministry program coordinated through their pastoral care department. Tom Stewart, Director of Pastoral Care, explains the purpose of this program, "The Clown Ministry at St. Luke's Hospital is a unique opportunity to blend the pastoral care skills of a compassionate caregiver with the entertainment skills of a clown. Clown ministers are invited to believe in the innate dignity of all human beings, and seek to understand and care for them as whole persons in terms of their relationship to God . . . Clown ministers use empathy and respect as the foundation for all interactions. As clowns, the Pastoral Care philosophy is expressed through the identity of their unique clown character and personality. Clowns are universal symbols of the child within all of us. The Clown gives everyone permission to become a child again, providing an invitation for the inner child to 'come out to play'. At times, this invitation is the only reprieve from life's daily hassles. Through articulating and acting out the ridiculous, the obvious, and the mundane details of life, a clown brings a welcome opportunity for the expression of love, joy, dignity, and laughter. They present themselves as symbols of God's love for all whom they come in contact" (Snowberg, 1992, pp. 102-103).

Sacred Clowns Of The Native Americans

Clowns have enhanced the sacred ceremonies of many cultures throughout history. They shock the audience with behaviors that are considered taboo, or actions that are backwards or contrary to expected behavior. Clowns capture the attention of the audience and allow them to forget petty concerns, opening them to a deeper experience.

Serious rituals or ceremonial dances demand intense concentration. The clown provides a comic interruption which shifts the structure of the ritual to reveal its deeper essence. It appears that the clowns are making fun of the ceremony by attempting to destroy it, but they are actually revealing a richer meaning for the observer.

In many Native American cultures, it is believed that certain ceremonies and rituals cannot be started until everyone present has started to laugh. Once people have laughed, they are prepared to participate in the sacred dimensions of the ritual. Some healing rituals are actually performed by clowns (Brown, 1979).

The Heyoka, Or Contrary

Among the Plains Indians, the Heyoka, or contrary, is a spiritual teacher as well as a trickster. To be a Heyoka requires an initial spiritual experience, usually in the form of a dream or vision. The sacred origin is essential, as the activities of a Heyoka are seen as a tool to communicate spiritual truths to the community. The Heyoka is expected to act in ways that break with the traditional norms of the tribe. They perform their activities in reverse: they place lodge poles on the outside of the tipi; they ride horses backward while shooting arrows over their shoulders; or they sit down with their feet up in the air while lying on their backs. These humorous antics of the Heyoka are meant to shatter a person's perception about everyday routines so that they may see things more objectively (Brown, 1979).

Black Elk was a Sioux Heyoka who told the story of several Heyokas who emerged from their tents after a brief rain shower. They saw a large, shallow puddle and became very excited about the possibility of a swim. They ran around the village until they found a long lodge pole. They hurried back to the puddle and carefully laid the pole across the puddle, measuring its width at about twenty feet, and marking the pole. They then took the pole and stood it upright, noting that the twenty foot mark was well above the tops of their heads. They all smiled and nodded at each other, agreeing that the puddle was sufficiently "deep" enough for them to swim in. With a great deal of noise and commotion to insure that everyone in camp was watching them, they stripped off their clothing down to their loin cloths, stood on the edge of the puddle, and dove head first into the shallow puddle. They hit their heads firmly on the earth and rolled around in mock pain and suffering. The observers, seeing the Heyoka's absurdly ridiculous logic and comical behavior laughed uproariously. And for that moment, they were cleansed of their worries and tensions.

The Heyoka actually perform contrary activities during sacred ceremonies. In Native American cultures, all shamans or Medicine Men have a medicine bundle which contains sacred items that are used to evoke the spirits and enhance the power of the healing ritual. The opening of the medicine bundle is an especially solemn moment, one of respect and reverence for the spirits. As a Heyoka, Black Elk would pause during the opening of the sacred medicine bundle and begin telling funny stories. Soon, everyone would be laughing and feeling more relaxed. Black Elk would then return to the sacred activity and begin the healing ritual. I shared this story at one of my workshops and a nurse related a similar incident that had occurred in the Cardiac Operating room where she worked. As the surgery team was preparing the many tubes and machines necessary for their "sacred healing," the surgeon asked if anyone had a new joke to share before they got started. After several jokes were shared and everyone had laughed, the team then focused intently on the five-hour operation they were ready to do.

Hopi Clowns

Long ago, according to Hopi mythology, the Hopi emerged from the underworld and wandered the earth with their gods, the Kachinas. During this time
they were attacked by Mexicans, and all the gods were killed. The dead gods
returned to the underworld, and the Hopi people divided their ceremonial
costumes and began to impersonate the gods. From then on, impersonating
Kachinas formed the core of Hopi rituals. When a man wore the sacred
costume of a Kachina, he became a friend of the gods (Bock, 1971;
Sekaquaptewa, 1979).

Sacred Kachina dances were held in the plaza formed by the pueblos of the
Hopi village. These dances lasted a full day, sometimes two. During a
particularly serious part of this sacred ceremony, the audience is distracted by
the noisy and sudden appearance of the Hopi clown Kachinas. Their bodies
are smeared with mud from the sacred springs, and on their heads they wear
improvised wigs made from stocking caps and corn husks.

The clowns pretend to step off the edge of the roof, one foot suspended in
midair, then retreat in mock fear, provoking uproarious laughter from the
spectators below, who quickly lose interest in the dancers. The clowns lower
a long plank to the ground and attempt to slide down head first. Considerable
horseplay follows, in which they pretend to lose their balance and tumble to
the ground. Parading around the plaza, the clowns suddenly feign great
surprise at seeing the Kachinas dancing, and they immediately join in. Showing little respect for the holiness of the occasion, they form their own dance
line aside the Kachinas, dancing out of step and even chanting irreverent
parodies of the Kachina songs. Inevitably, their clumsy, shuffling motions
deteriorate into a shoving contest in which the clowns fall all over one
another. When a clown feels tired he sits on the ground and rocks stupidly
back and forth, peering foolishly at onlookers. Sometimes he dashes into the
crowd, teasing the children, taunting the adults, and stealing objects. When
the dance is complete, he obliviously continues dancing, and upon discovering that the other dancers have exited, races after them. Similar "blow off"
or exit routines are used by circus clowns today!

Healing Clowns

Among the Iroquois, the False Face Society was a group organized to counteract the Evil Spirit and his emissaries. Their duties included curing illness and keeping evil spirits at bay. When someone in the village was ill, the members gathered and covered themselves with face masks, blankets and carried turtle-shell rattles. The masks were inspired by mythological beings and creatures seen during dreams. A mask was carved from a living basswood tree and portrayed different facial types. The most distinguishing features were crooked mouths, smiles, or protruding tongues. These clowns were believed to have the ability to heal by performing a comic exorcism of the demons who caused illness.

The clown-healers would arrive at the lodge of the sick person and begin to dance around the room. They would crawl on the floor and behave like children, kicking, whining and begging for food. Sometimes they would talk in strange nonsense languages. The sick person would howl with laughter at their comical antics. At times, the clowns performed what seemed to be magical feats. They would remove hot coals from the fire, dance around, hooting and jumping while juggling the hot coals with their bare hands. Finally, they would rub ashes onto the head of the sick person, offer a blessing to be healed, and then leave (Towsen, 1976).

The Zuni nation occupies a region just west of the Continental Divide in western New Mexico. The town of Zuni is the central hub of the reservation today. A 'Newekwe' is a Zuni clown Kachina and modern day healer who belongs to a healing society. To gain membership in one of these societies, a person must be cured of a stomach aliment by a Newekwe clown. To ensure that the cure is permanent, they must be initiated into the clown society. According to Zuni belief, worry resides in the stomach and is the primary cause of illness. Before their performances, the clowns are reminded by their leaders to "make your mind blank" and to "go out there with a happy heart, a heart free from worry, and help the people" (Stevenson, 1904; Benedict, 1935; Tedlock, 1978).

In 1879, Frank Cushing, a naturalist with no training in anthropology, was sent to the Territory of New Mexico by the Bureau of American Ethnology. He was to inquire first hand into the customs and beliefs of the Zuni. Frank lived among the Indians for almost five years. He shared in their activities, mastered their language, received instruction in their myths and rituals, and grew to understand the complex organization of their society as no other non-Indian had ever done. In one of his reports he describes the Zuni clown, Newekwe, who has the ability to eat any amount of food or garbage.

"I have seen a Newekwe gather about him his melons, green and ripe, raw peppers, bits of stick and refuse... in fact, anything soft enough or small enough to be forced down his gullet... and with the greatest apparent gusto, consume them all at a single sitting. Once after such a repast, two of these Ne'we... fixed their staring eyes on me, and motioned me to give them something else to eat! I ran home, caught up some crackers, threw them onto some paper, and in order to make them relish the better, poured a pint or two of molasses over them. I wrapped an old woolen army jacket around this... hurried back [and] cast the bundle into the plaza. The pair immediately fell to fighting for its possession, consequently broke the paper, scattered some of the crackers about the ground and daubed the back of the coat with the molasses. They gathered up the fragments of crackers and ate them... then fought over the paper and ate that, and finally tore pieces out of the back of the coat with their teeth and ate them (though it nearly choked them to do so) after which the victor put the coat on and triumphantly wore it, his painted skin showing like white patches through the holes he had bitten in the back of the coat" (Cushing, 1920, pp. 621-622).

On July 20, 1969, the first man walked on the moon, and the Zuni faced a threat to their religious beliefs. The sacred Moon Mother, ultimate source of all light and life, had been violated by two white men who removed nearly fifty pounds of her flesh without so much as a prayer. This was a profound religious shock to the Zuni people. For the next ten years, the Newekwe performed skits that negated both the religious threat and scientific seriousness of the lunar landing. During the Kachina dances, the clowns would dress up like rockets and satellites and run madly around the village, then crash and roll over feigning dead in front of the dancers. Their goal was to startle and shock the audience into laughing or at least gasping their disapproval. The Zuni audiences were finally able to laugh at the absurdity of space exploration. The Zuni clowns see boundaries as challenging hurdles. By helping others to laugh, they share a moment of detachment and remove the very worry that their people believe is the source of disease (Tedlock, 1979).

To become conscious of what is horrifying and to laugh at it, is to become master of what is horrifying. The comic alone is capable of giving us the strength to bear the tragedy of existence.

—Eugene Ionesco

Sacred and healing clowns are still seen today in modern hospitals and community churches. The Caring Clown hospital visitation program and many Clown Ministry groups in churches continue these ancient traditions. But before we explore these groups, let us first examine the essence and spirit of the clown.

A Message from Nancy Nurse

I believe the essence of the clown is innocence and vulnerability. Clowns approach life with the simple innocence of a child. Everything, no matter how small, is a wondrous surprise. We find great delight in the discovery of something new, and see everything as if it were for the first time. Clowns don't have any expectations or preconceptions of what might happen, and because of that, every moment has endless possibilities. Like a child, the clown believes that everyone is good. In our innocence and trust, we are willing to take risks and always say, "Yes—yes, of course, I'll jump off that cliff."

Vulnerability is an essential quality for any clown. Our vulnerability makes us accessible, lovable and open. When we are vulnerable, we allow things to happen, because we don't need to be in control. We are open and sensitive to our own emotions and express them with our entire being—body, mind and spirit. Clowns are sensitive to the feelings and needs of others, and reflect that sensitivity in their choice of responses (Bain, 1993).

The spirit of the clown is, of course, love. First, we must love ourselves, accepting our own weaknesses and imperfections, acknowledging our foolishness. Clowns radiate love towards others. We accept people just as they are, and honor their personal space. We remain sensitive to everyone we encounter, reading their non-verbal cues, and responding with kindness and love.

The Clown

> *The genius of clowning is transforming the little,*
> *everyday annoyances, not only overcoming,*
> *but actually transforming them into something strange*
> *and terrific... it is the power to extract mirth for millions*
> *out of nothing and less than nothing.*

> —*'Grock' (Wettach, 1969)*

The clown shows us just how awkward being a human can be. He or she is always eager and hopeful but often, does not succeed. The clown meets each failure with a grin or a shrug, forgets the past and moves on to the next disaster. Through the clown, we recognize our own vulnerability, yet we feel inspired by his resilience and courage. The clown is both pathetic and lovable and we laugh, because the clown is one of us. The clown combines both the essence of the mythical trickster and the archetypal fool into one playful and resilient character that celebrates all of life.

Whiteface

The white-faced clown, commonly called the Pierott, has many characteristics of the trickster. He is both clever and awkward yet, always in complete control. The make-up style, as the name implies, is entirely white. Small amounts of color or glitter are used to express the features of the eyes, nose, and mouth. The hair is covered with a white skull cap and topped with a small cone shaped hat. The costume is stylish and elegant, usually a one piece jumpsuit with sequins, pom-pom buttons, ruffles, flared pants, and long sleeves. Ballet or dancing shoes are worn instead of large comedy shoes. The character of the white-faced clown is reserved, sophisticated and gentle. This clown type is more likely to throw the pie than receive it. Famous white-faced clowns include Pierott of 18th century France, and Joseph Grimaldi, the famous English clown of the early 1800's (Manning-Sanders, 1952; Wettach, 1957; Speaight, 1980).

Grimaldi's clown was a delightfully roguish character who could not resist a chance to steal, especially when it came to his favorite foods: sausages and pies. His make-up was the typical white face of the Pierott, but with larger splashes of color on his cheeks, mouth and eyebrows. His costume varied considerably, especially when he was out to satirize the latest in fashion. Grimaldi was a master of pantomime and especially of facial grimaces. As one of his fans described him, "He was a master of grimace; and whether he was robbing a pieman, opening an oyster, devouring a pudding or picking a pocket, he was so extravagantly natural. His expression was in his face and body, even his nose was capable of exhibiting disdain, fear, anger and even joy" (Manning-Sanders, 1952, p. 48). His routines often contained political satire. He poked fun at the extravagant finery of military officers by using two black coal buckets as his boots, real horseshoes on his heels, and, chains and large brass dishes as spurs, making it so that he cluttered and clattered as he walked! (Towsen, 1976).

Auguste

The Auguste clown is both clumsy and impish. The word "Auguste" means stupid. Whatever the task at hand, the Auguste clown will exert a tremendous amount of misguided energy and accomplish very little! His methods are inappropriate and his failure inevitable. The make-up for the Auguste clown is highly colorful. Designs around the eyes and mouth are usually red or black. The Auguste will always wear a huge wig, and usually dons a large comical nose. His costume is a tailor's nightmare with colorful, often mismatched accessories. Jacket and pants are usually too big or too small, complimented by large collars, suspenders, and of course the traditional oversized clown shoes. Famous Auguste clowns include Grock, a Swiss clown of the early 1900's, and Lou Jacobs, a Ringling Brothers circus clown from 1924-1955 (Towsen, 1976; Bain, 1993).

Jacobs would enter the circus ring attired in a hunting jacket and carrying a rifle. He was followed by his tiny dog, Knucklehead, who was disguised as a rabbit with the addition of artificial bunny ears. Jacobs' points his rifle at imaginary ducks flying about, but much to his frustration, they all seem to flutter away before he can take precise aim.

As he stalks his game, he spots the 'rabbit.' Excited by an easy catch, he carefully takes aim. His faithful dog sits up on its hind legs. He shoots and the 'rabbit' falls over. Quite pleased with himself, Jacobs deposits the 'rabbit' in his pouch, which, however, is really a bottomless sack through which a very alive rabbit-dog escapes. Confused, Jacobs again stalks his game, shoots it, and drops it in his bag. Again it escapes and once more, the baffled clown prepares to shoot the rabbit.

But now he realized there is something peculiar about this animal. He takes a closer look and his frustration quickly turns to shame when he pulls off its ears and discovers he has been trying to murder his own best friend. Eager to make amends, Jacobs tries to pick up Knucklehead, but the dog is not inclined to forgive him so easily. It deftly eludes his grasp. He gives chase, but Knucklehead runs circles around him. Visibly upset, he throws his hat to the ground . . . and Knucklehead picks it up and runs off. Jacobs has to get down on his hands and knees and beg before Knucklehead will return the cap and forgive him, and a happy reunion concludes the piece (Towsen, 1976).

Clowns remind us that we can play with our existence and perceive words, things, and circumstances in many ways. The clown's act teaches us how a disaster can be transformed into a simple comic inconvenience. As we laugh we feel empowered, for how can anything overwhelm us if we can make fun of it? When the sad-faced Emmett Kelly is incapable of performing even the simplest task, like sweeping the floor, or when Buster Keaton stares in blank resignation at the collapsed house to which he has just given a final hammer blow, we laugh! We laugh because similar misfortunes have happened to us, leaving us feeling similarly helpless. We laugh because we are capable of taking even the most painful situations and translating them differently. We can always laugh! (Hyers, 1996).

Tramp Or Character Clown

The Tramp was born in response to the American depression when tramps and hobos were commonplace. The tramp often wears a forlorn expression and his make-up usually gives him an unshaven appearance. The costume is patched and ragged and reflects the reality of depression life. We identify with him, as both he and his situation are so obviously human. This clown type brought a whole new style to circus clowning. Up until then, most clowns performed at a great distance from their audience, arriving in a large group to run about in wild abandon, before chasing one another out of the ring. The Tramp, however, wanders around on his own, interacting with individual members of the audience. It is rare for a smile to play across his lips, for he has nothing to smile about. His actions are deliberate, his manner gentle, his response usually bewildered, and his air, one of great solemnity. We find him excruciatingly funny because he continues to be absolutely serious about everything he tries to do, no matter how futile or foolish it appears to be (Towsen, 1976; Bain, 1993).

Emmett Kelly's character, "Weary Willie," is perhaps one of the most memorable Tramp clowns. With his sad and forlorn expression, he would wander through the audience carrying a cabbage. After a while, he would make eye contact with one woman in the audience and become enamored with her. He would act as though he had fallen madly in love. He would approach her shyly and then offer her his most treasured possession, his cabbage. Kelly would play off her response, much to the delight of the audience. Finally, when she was not thrilled with either him or his gift, he would shrug his shoulders and wander off, looking for another woman to love.

As Kelly described his character, "I am a sad and ragged little guy, who is very serious about everything... I am the hobo who found out the hard way that the deck is stacked, the dice 'frozen,' the race fixed, and the wheel crooked, but there is always present, that one tiny forlorn spark of hope still glimmering in his soul, which makes him keep on trying (Kelly, 1954, pp. 125-126).

By laughing at me, the audience really laughs at themselves and realizing they have done this, gives them a sort of spiritual second wind for going back into the battle of life.

—Emmett Kelly

The essence of Clowning does not lie in make-up, costume, or shtick (performance), but rather in the quality of compassion and sensitivity that the clown offers to the audience. John Towsen, clown historian and performer, received his Ph.D. from New York University in Drama with a doctoral thesis on the evolution of clowning. He speaks of Otto Griebling's (an American tramp clown) perspective on clowning, "If you find yourself able to make people laugh, it is God's gift. You have to do everything from the bottom of your heart. I let the emotion come from inside and penetrate the eyes. I'm the same man underneath, I'm always part of the human tragi-comedy" (Cline, 1983, p. 46).

The clown helps us to see ourselves, recognize the folly of our situation, and then forgive ourselves for not being quite perfect. The clown restores the sense of wonder and mystery that scientific society undermines. We need the clown now more than ever before!

Dimitri, a Swiss who was born in 1935, created a naive, childlike clown character, a very serious chap who could not keep his hands off all the delicious temptations that surrounded him. As a railroad station porter, he delights in opening all the luggage he transports. He experiments with the wonderful musical instruments he discovers inside. He uses a variety of techniques, most of them wrong, to play the guitar... At one point he swallows a harmonica and then regurgitates three bite-sized harmonicas. Every new object presents a challenge, to be met full-force with his typical eccentric manner. Dimitri is like a little boy trying out a new toy for the first time, and when it works he is just as thrilled and surprised as we are! (Towsen, 1976).

Modern Clowns

A painted face is not always necessary to identify a clown. Both Charlie Chaplin and Buster Keaton were clowns. Character comedians such as Lily Tomlin, Robin Williams, and Victor Borge employed clowning techniques and antics to develop their characters.

On his video-taped performance, "Live at the Met," we watch Robin Williams enact the probable scene that would occur if a ballet choreographer changed positions with a football coach. At first, Williams portrays the effeminate director, who swishes about on stage, encouraging the linebackers to, "Push, Push, Push, big boys!" Then he enacts the gruff and demanding football coach barking out orders to the ballet troupe, "Okay now, Barishnikov, I want you to go long, and wait for someone to throw Giselle, and remember, the game ain't over 'till the swan takes it in the ass" (See Humor Resource List).

Lily Tomlin is a master of character development. In her one woman show, "Signs of Intelligent Life," she has created multiple characters with an incredible range of personalities. She performs them all impeccably, from the homespun Kentucky couple, Lud and Marie, to Agnes Angst, a severely disturbed punk rocker, to Trudy, the bag lady with her umbrella hat through which she receives messages from extra terrestrials. On the TV show, Saturday Night Live, Tomlin captured the hearts of Americans with her portrayal of the no-nonsense telephone operator, Ernestine. Snorting and clucking at her switchboard while connecting a call, "One ringy-dingy. Two ringy-dingy," we all laughed and forgot our own ridiculous mannerisms.

The Whiteface and Auguste clowns often worked together as a team, with the Whiteface trickster pulling the chair out from under the foolish Auguste. This juxtaposition of straight man and buffoon is still portrayed in the comedy teams of modern time. Oliver Hardy was plump and domineering, Stan Laurel was skinny and brow beaten. Mae West was a seductive, aloof beauty. W. C. Fields was the alcoholic, cigar puffing scalawag. Dean Martin was the handsome lady's man and Jerry Lewis was the awkward, bungling kid. George Burns was the clever and perceptive gentleman and Gracie Allen was his simple and easily confused wife. Abbott, the straight man and Costello, the fool. Working together as teams, these modern clowns increased the impact and hilarity of their routines.

Caring Clowns

Clowns bring joy and delight to people who suffer. Clowns are a part of healing rituals and today many are called, "Caring Clowns." They perform in hospitals, nursing homes and health care facilities. As we discussed in Chapter Four, Caring Clowns are employed by hospitals throughout the US to continue an ancient tradition. They provide a service to patients, their families and hospital staff.

The scene is an Outpatient Clinic where several young, frightened children with leukemia await chemotherapy. The children are all thin and pale, their bald heads covered with baseball caps. Enter three strange 'doctors' in white lab coats. Instead of the usual fear and tension that arises when specialists stride into the waiting room, there are howls of laughter as this funny trio produces soap bubbles, hand puppets, magic tricks, juggling balls and general merriment.

These 'doctors of delight' are a group of caring clowns from the Big Apple Circus at the Clown Care Unit in New York City. This clown visitation program began as a five week experimental project at Babies Hospital of the Columbia Presbyterian Medical Center in New York City. The Big Apple Circus - Clown Care Unit now employs more than 30 clowns who perform at many city hospitals. These clowns are polished performers even before they take the additional training required to become a Caring Clown.

The clowns attempt to make hospital procedures less frightening by poking gentle fun at them. They entertain with giant squirting syringes and stethoscopes with bubbles coming out one end. Martin Nash, M.D., Director of Pediatric Nephrology at Babies Hospital says, "The clowns do a tremendous amount to reduce the fear in both kids and their families. They're remarkable at breaking down barriers" (Darrach, 1990, p. 77).

The success of the program depends on the sensitivity of the performers to the moods and needs of their young patients. These clowns perform in pairs, allowing them to play their comedy off each other rather than depending on the patient's ability to interact. As the two clowns enter the Clinic, the music from their squeeze box captures the kids' attention. When they spot the clowns, their eyes get as big as saucers, and big grins spread across their faces. One clown offers a mother a "red nose transplant," and when she accepts, the kids squeal with delight at seeing the clown nose on Mom's face. Next the clowns blow bubbles and challenge the kids to catch the bubbles on their noses. This is followed by an amazing juggling routine where the clowns actually take bites from the apples while they are juggling them. During the clown visit, peals of laughter and giggles pour out from the clinic and the smiles they have stimulated last for the rest of the day. The Big Apple Circus - Caring Clown Care Unit is the largest and most well developed clown visitation program in America. They are producing a training program and handbook to help others develop their skills and expertise as Caring Clowns.

Children's Hospital in Winnipeg, Canada is a very busy place. Children come from throughout the province for special procedures and intricate surgeries. When the children arrive, they are frightened by the large hospital, the strange people and the unusual equipment. It is important for the medical staff to build trust and communication with the children as quickly as possible so they may begin the necessary procedures. Children's Hospital has found a unique and effective way to help with that transition.

Hubert, the staff clown, works closely with the nursing and medical staff to build trust between the physicians and patients. The doctors frequently play off the clown to establish better communication. The children feel empowered if they can help Hubert tie his shoelace or adjust his crooked hat. They become caregivers too, instead of merely care receivers. Ellen Good, Director the hospital's Child Life Program, describes clowning as a universal language that instantly cuts across all cultural and national barriers and speaks directly to the heart. The clowning program has been so successful that the Child Life Program has produced a series of video tapes starring Robo, a former hospital clown. These tapes are available for purchase and help prepare children for shots, X-rays, removal of a cast and other procedures. They even have a video tape that offer guidance in setting up a pediatric clown program (See Humor Resource List). If you are interested in learning clown skills, you must first find your own unique, clown 'self.' Discovering your inner clown is a good exercise whether you plan to 'clown around' or just learn more about yourself!

The Inner Clown

For several years now, the clown has taken on great importance.... as part of the search for what is laughable and ridiculous in man. We [should] put the emphasis on the rediscovery of our own individual clown, the one that has grown-up within us and which society does not allow us to express.

—Jacques Lequoc (1973)

Each of us has a little clown inside us just waiting to pop out and express itself in a fun way. By finding your own inner clown—the fool in yourself, you can learn to play with life and joke about anything and everything. As the energy of your inner clown is released, it must be captured in a well defined character. All of your actions, responses, thoughts and feelings are projected to your audience through your clown character. Developing a character takes time and practice. You must know what motivates your clown to make your actions believable. Ask yourself these questions about your character: What does your character want? What will they do to get it? A strong character is essential for great clowning and it reduces the awkward feelings that can arise when the situation doesn't go according to plan (Stolzenberg, 1981).

Developing Your Clown Character

When I developed my latest clown character, "Nurse Kindheart" I worked with a highly skilled trainer and talented performer, Arina Isaacson. Arina runs the San Francisco Clown School (See Humor Resource List) and teaches a variety of training formats in her studio as well as instructing at Clown Camp. Arina is a gentle, yet demanding character coach, and she helped me find "Nurse Kindheart's" clown walk, hand movements, posture, and gestures that would embody the qualities of her character and make my clown believable.

The hard work paid off a few months later when I was performing before an audience of 500 nurses on the opening night of the Journal of Nursing Jocularity Conference. I was seated on stage giving "report," a mostly verbal routine with an accompanying slide show. Within the course of five minutes, it seemed that everything that could go wrong, went wrong. The house lights when on and off at wrong times, a helium balloon drifted in front of the slide projector, my reading light on stage went out and left me in the dark. You name it, it went wrong. But, because my character was strong and I was immersed in "being that character," I was able to spontaneously create comical ad lib's, much to the delight of the audience and to the relief of Doug Fletcher, the conference coordinator and publisher of the *Journal of Nursing Jocularity.*

When the lights went out at the wrong moment, "Nurse Kindheart" requested, "Could the dear, sweet person who did that, please place your hand back on the switch and do it the other way again?" When the balloon floated in front of the slide projector, she calmly remarked, "Well, now, it appears we're having an eclipse." And when all the house lights went out, leaving "Nurse Kindheart" completely in the dark, and the audience gasping in sympathetic pain for my predicament, she commented, "Don't worry dearies, I've done enough night shifts to be able to figure things out in the dark. Do you suppose this is why Florence advised us to always carry the lamp?"

People tell me they feel so much more available to life once they learn how to clown around.
That's what being a clown is about . . . it's about touching your soul and finally giving it room to laugh.

—Arina Issacson

My Inner Clown is Born

I discovered my first inner clown in 1973. I was recovering from a painful divorce. I was lonely, my heart ached, and even after a year, I still had crying spells. I was trying to provide a loving home for my one-year old son. Ken was a bright and playful toddler who greeted each day as early as he could, usually awakening by seven in the morning. This was much too early for me. I usually got to bed about 3 AM after getting off the evening shift, driving to the baby-sitter's to get Ken, and then driving home again. Seven AM was much, much too early to awaken, but as every mother knows, your day begins when your kids get up. My mornings were always busy with household chores, a trip to the park, and then I was off to work at 1:30 PM at University Hospital.

I felt tired before I even started my shift in a busy ICU for neurologically damaged patients. The next nine hours were spent caring for young victims of motorcycle accidents who weren't wearing helmets, elderly people who suffered a massive strokes with internal hemorrhaging into the brain, and people of all ages with cancerous brain tumors. I would care for these often comatose patients, comfort their families, and try to help the new interns learn something about our care protocols in the unit. Everywhere I looked, both inside and out, I saw pain, suffering, sadness, and loss. The joyful spirit, which usually filled my inner being, was gone. I knew that I had to rediscover my happiness, or be sucked into a black hole of depression and hopelessness.

One day, while driving to work, a radio announcement caught my attention. A very happy voice seemed to speak directly to me! The voice announced a new "clownology" course that was being offered by the San Diego State University extension program. I began to hope that this clown training might help me rediscover that joyful spirit I had lost through the last year of losses. I called the college the next morning and without hesitation, enrolled in the fourteen week course. Rich Wise, a Ringling Brothers Clown College graduate, taught the course. His enthusiasm and playfulness inspired us to push past the hesitation we all felt about becoming foolish. Together, with fifteen other adults, I learned how to apply make-up, design costumes, develop a character, and perform funny magic tricks and skit routines.

I'll never forget putting on my make up for my first performance in Balboa Park. At one point I almost panicked, thinking, "What if they don't think I'm funny?" How humiliating! I had to stop and reassure myself that first of all, the audience wouldn't know who I really was, and furthermore, how could I expect to be confident until I got a little practice under my belt? As it turned out, everything went pretty well, though I noted plenty of room for improvement. Soon I was able to "clown around" in parades, at birthday parties, or walking around the park.

I remember my first parade. I had decided to wear my roller skates so that I could preserve my precious energy and still "work the crowd" on both sides of the street through the whole parade route. Before the parade started, I registered and claimed my preassigned number in the line-up and then skated back to my place in line. My excitement grew as I spotted the group assigned to proceed me in the parade — it was a man and his elephant, and the elephant had on roller skates. As I skated through the parade, I'd pause and ask the audience, "Have you see my mother? She's big and fat, has a long nose, and is wearing roller skates!"

Clowning was fun and I began to feel better. Clowning taught me that I had the ability and flexibility to change the way I looked at life. I could choose to view my life as depressing and serious, trying in vain to control the people and circumstances around me, or, I could choose to distort my problems and see them in outrageous and comical proportions. My inner clown taught me how to laugh and play again. And I had to do that, if I was to remain physically and mentally healthy.

Scruffy the Clown is Born

My first clown character was Scruffy, a sad-faced tramp clown. At first, my make-up was reddish with a gray wig, but I noticed that kids were afraid of him. I think the make-up and wig colors were too depressing. Also, my sad mouth was turned downward too severely and didn't change when I smiled. Then I purchased an orange yak fur wig (the finest type you can buy!) and changed my make-up to orange, and the smile to one whose expression could quickly change into delight upon discovering someone to play and laugh with. After a few years, Scruffy began visiting nursing homes, bringing the gift of laughter to the elderly. I saw how quickly they were able to access their inner child and become playful. As I would walk down the halls of the nursing home, the residents would clap their hands excitedly and announce, "The circus has come to town!" They would reach out to touch me and laughed and smiled. The staff said they'd never seen some of those residents smile before my visit. They assured me that after my clown visit, the residents had much more energy, better appetites and were more open to interaction with others. Wow! I was funny—and, even better, I was making a difference in someone's life!

My Humor Career is Born

I became curious if anyone else had noticed the healing effect of clowning on the elderly, so I did some research at the library. I found several books describing how laughter and clowns could stimulate healing. One of those books was, *Anatomy of an Illness,* by Norman Cousins. As I read those first few pages, I felt a career emerging! I became excited at the possibilities of using the very skill I had learned for my own healing and happiness to help others. But could I make a living at it?

I began to explore ways that nursing and my clowning could be combined. I began by performing and speaking to nursing students at a nearby community college. We discussed the importance of maintaining our sense of humor in order to survive the many challenges and stresses of the nursing profession. I spoke about mental, spiritual, and physical health, and how they were dependent on our ability to maintain a balance between the intense tragedy we witness as caregivers, and the joy and satisfaction we receive when we can help someone. One of the student nurses in my class became excited about our discussions, and she ran home and told her mother, an RN (real nurse), about my performance and my message. Later that month, I was invited to speak to the nursing staff at her mother's hospital. And the rest, as they say, is history. My new career catapulted forward.

In 1983, I started my own business, "Jest for the Health of It!" I developed several workshops and presentations for nurses so that they could receive continuing education credit for therapeutic humor training. After a few years, I began developing a product line of books and toys. For the last 12 years, I have presented workshops, lectures, and seminars throughout the United States, Canada, and in Europe! Many experiences stand out in my memory as I look over my years of leading workshops, but one is especially vivid.

It happened in Los Angeles. One hospital sponsored my workshop and invited nurses from nearby hospitals to attend, so there were about two hundred nurses in the room. Everything went smoothly during the morning sessions, and after lunch I appeared for my "Nancy Nurse" performance. Now, most clowns have been taught to "play off" the people that laugh the most. These people are somehow connected to your character in a vital way and will continue to laugh, even louder, if you play to them. One silver-haired nurse sitting near the front row was laughing so hard, she was crying. The more she laughed, the more I fed her lines, and the more she laughed.

I was so involved, I didn't notice several other people watching us in gasping disbelief. During the break, a few people approached me to announce they'd just witnessed a miracle. They explained that the woman who was laughing uncontrollably had recently retired from her faculty position at a nearby nursing school. For 25 years she had taken student nurses for their clinical assignments to the hospitals where many of the workshop participants worked. The miracle? Nobody, in the past 25 years had *ever* heard this woman laugh, much less smile. In that moment, I was absolutely certain I was doing the work God meant for me to do.

> *For what, after all, is the laughter a good clown brings us*
> *but the giddiness that comes from suddenly seeing,*
> *as if from a cosmic viewpoint, the absurdity of what*
> *the mighty are up to? For that moment,*
> *we taste the sanity of divine madness, and become,*
> *for as long as the joke lasts, fools of God.*
>
> *—Theodore Rozak*

As I grew and changed, so did my inner clown. I decided that if nurses were going to see the comedy inherent in their profession, it would help if they could identify with a "nurse clown." This wacky character could comically distort the professional's reality, revealing the humor beneath the job and the potential for folly. So, in 1984 my second clown was born.

Nancy Nurse Is Born

"Nancy Nurse" is a wild, red-headed clown, armed with a combat belt of weapons such as, bedpans, urinals, enema buckets, and over-sized syringes used to fight diseases. Her stethoscope is made from a garden hose and a toilet plunger which is great to use on those big-hearted patients... it can also be used to relieve constipation! "Nancy Nurse" is bold, outspoken, and in control of both patients and doctors. Nurses love her outrageous solutions to common problems. She promises the uncooperative patient a '5 H' enema: High, Hot, a Hell of a lot, and Hold it 'till it Hurts!

She manages a demanding patient with simple clown logic. If your patient is annoying you by constantly putting on their call light, you have several choices to remove this irritation. One, you can ignore it, but usually the light above the door continues to flash and the bell at the nursing station keeps ringing, announcing to everyone that you are a negligent, uncaring nurse— not a good idea if you want to get promoted. Second solution: you render the patient unconscious with drugs or a physical therapy intervention (therapy for the nurse). But we know nurses can't give drugs without a physician's order and you'll never find a doc to write one for the amount of sedation you really want to give the patient, and the physical intervention is another nix because of that pesky little assault and battery law. So, the only choice you really have is number three. Go in the patient's room and ever so gently and quietly remove the call light from the bedside rail and place it under the mattress. Then act completely surprised if anyone ever finds out!

Through "Nancy Nurse," caregivers learn to laugh at themselves and gain some distance from the serious and tragic aspects of the profession. "Nancy Nurse" performs a stage show primarily for audiences of health professionals. But over the years, she began to speak to patient support groups after the workshops with nurses.

Sometimes "Nancy Nurse" was asked to make "clown rounds" at hospitals to entertain patients. I learned that the character of "Nancy Nurse" was not as funny to patients, and that some were actually frightened by her presence. "Nancy Nurse" was too big, bold, and boisterous for the delicate art of bedside clowning. I needed another clown for patients and their families—a clown that was gentle, kind, and concerned for the patient and their vulnerable situation.

Nurse Kindheart Is Born

My third clown was born in 1994. "Nurse Kindheart" is a dear, sweet, white-haired, proper nurse with a clipped British accent who embodies all the old fashioned qualities of nursing that are sometimes lost among the technology and bustling activity of the hospital. "Nurse Kindheart" is patient and reassuring as she clucks, "There, there dear, let me fix you a good, hot cup of tea and we'll talk about this problem and solve it together." She is a devoted patient advocate, protecting them from interruption during their naps. She also checks the doctor's malpractice insurance coverage to verify that it is sufficient.

"Nurse Kindheart" embodies the qualities of compassion and sensitivity that all patients need and that most nurses still value. The techniques of Western allopathic medicine place great demands upon the professional nurse today. Sophisticated monitoring equipment, complex medication procedures and intricate infection control policies create multiple distractions for any professional caregiver. The home care environment is beginning to look more and more like a hospital room, as patients are being discharged "quicker and sicker." Several nurse educators are helping nurses to remember just how important compassion and caring are for both the patient and the nurse (See Appendix).

"Nurse Kindheart" offers a gentle reminder to all caregivers, to be gentle, patient and kind in every contact they have with patients, family and colleagues. "Nurse Kindheart" is the antithesis of "Nancy Nurse." "Nancy" is wild and crazy, bold and brash, oversized and noisy. "Nurse Kindheart" is a true "Angel of Mercy." She is sweet and demure, careful and polite, refined and serene. "Nurse Kindheart" believes that LOVE is the greatest healing energy there is so she exudes this to everyone she meets.

Her uniform is crisp and professional, with long sleeves and a pleated bodice (she would never wear "scrubs"). Her hose are white (of course) and she wears sensible duty shoes. Small, pink heart-shaped buttons run the length of her uniform and her shoes display a large pink heart and pink shoelaces. A pink nurse's cap sits atop her snow-white hair, which is loosely tied into a bun. And, on the tip of her nose is a small pink, heart-shaped clown nose, so when she "sticks her nose into other people's business," they know she loves them.

Being an old fashioned nurse, "Nurse Kindheart" realizes the importance of being present and available. She frequently visits her patients to provide peace and comfort. She queries their physicians about the completeness of their orders and insures that they have anticipated any problems her patients might have before their next visit. After all, she tells the doctors, "I wouldn't want to disturb you late at night with my questions, dearie. You look so weary, you deserve a good nights' sleep and maybe a wee sip of sherry to insure sweet dreams." "Nurse Kindheart" remembers the good old days when nurses cared for patients in large wards filled with ten or twenty beds. It was much easier to help each other back then, when several nurses worked together in one big room. Today, with all these private rooms and specialty units, it requires greater effort for nurses to stay in touch and help each other during the shift.

Recently, I spoke at the Maine State Nurses Association. At the last minute, I offered to bring "Nurse Kindheart" to the luncheon and they agreed. As I entered the room in my costume, they mentioned, "Oh, by the way, the President of the American Association of Nurses, Virginia Betts, is here. She'll be speaking after lunch." "Nurse Kindheart" immediately said, "Oh my dear, the Queen of Nursing herself. Well, I've got a message for her straight from Florence." As I walked toward the head table to deliver that message, I didn't know exactly what I would say to this prestigious spokesperson for nursing. I stopped to glance at a program and noticed her topic was "Cutbacks in Healthcare—How to Survive." I tried to imagine what my character believed about Health Care Reform. Just as I arrived at her table, the message came to me. After some brief chatting, I told her my message from Flo. "Florence wanted me to tell you why nurses are called 'Angels of Mercy.' It's because everyone expects us to do everything on just a wing and a prayer." Ginny was delighted and later incorporated that comment into her speech.

INNER CLOWNS SPEAK OUT

Each of my inner clowns has a unique perspective on life. Listen while they share that vision and tell you why they came to me when I needed my "inner jester."

Scruffy

"Life is not always fair, and sometimes you don't get what you want. You can't let that stop you from having fun. And you can't just sit around and wait for fun to find YOU. When you start to have fun, you can 'turn your frown upside down.' It happens to me. When I'm not having any fun, I look sad and forlorn, I feel lonely and hopeless. Once I start having some fun, everything changes and I know that I can survive anything. When I first met Patty, she was one of the most forlorn people I'd ever seen. Her frown was so down it touched the ground. I couldn't bear to see her that way, so I decided to teach her my ideas about fun. Together, with her son Ken, we helped her discover her playful inner child. Soon she was laughing again and her frown had turned upside down. I knew she would remember the skills I taught her and use them if she ever got stuck again."

Nancy Nurse

"Hey, nursing ain't easy, in fact, life ain't easy. But, you can't let reality ruin your day. Sometimes you've gotta "shift your wit" so you don't have to do it the other way around. Yeah, yeah, I know, patient's whine, doctor's bark, and those blasted "bean counters" from administration are always trying to claim more power over patient care decisions. Well, I say, its time to deal with it! Ignoring it won't help, and I doubt that anybody's going to change. So, here's my plan....

If your patient whines like a puppy, then treat 'em like a puppy. Really! Think about it, what do you do if a puppy whines? You pick them up and love 'em and pet 'em and maybe play with them a little. You check to make sure they don't really need to go to the bathroom and you see if they're hungry or in pain. If nothing's wrong, then just assure them that they are safe. Tell 'em to go to sleep and have some exciting puppy dreams. Maybe even give 'em a hot water bottle to cuddle up next to. But don't, I repeat, DON'T take them into bed with you. Once you do that, they're gonna want to sleep with you for the rest of your life!

Now doctors are a different story. The bad news is, unlike the patients' that get better and go away, the doctors keep coming back day after day. The good news is, once you get 'em trained, your life's a whole lot easier. Doctors have always barked at nurses. Don't ask me why, it's kinda like gravity, you can depend on it. Breeds of doctors are just like other breeds of barking species. Some of them are the yappy, nippy kind that start runnin' around in circles when something gets 'em riled up. Others are the mournful howlers—if they want something they don't have, they tilt their head back and howl. It's kinda spooky when that happens during night shift with a full moon. Still other doctors are the ones that snarl and growl. They try to dominate the neighborhood with intimidating behavior.

Of course, there are the kind we all love, the cute and cuddly tail waggers that will fetch a chart for you. This type will never chew up your shoes and they are completely housebroken. They don't bark or whine when you're not there, but they're always glad to see you return. This is the type you want to breed (not personally mind you). Put this type in the middle of the whole pack and then praise them, and perhaps the others will notice and change their behavior. It's worth a try. To reform this pack of wild dogs will take some perseverance and courage, so here's my next plan...

For the yippers, try saying "Bad dog. Sit and stay." If that doesn't work, you may have to isolate them in a room away from all the excitement. If your dog of the day starts to howl, sit down next to them and howl right along with them. Howling together unifies the pack, its a way of belonging to the group. Usually, though, this type of howler prefers to be heard alone and may resent your howling intrusion. They will probably just go somewhere else to howl. The ones that snarl and growl are the scariest. It can be so bad that sometimes you begin to wonder about their rabies vaccination. Forget the "Bad Dog" or "Down Boy" commands, they rarely respond. The best approach is to snarl back. That's right, assert yourself, claim your turf, and let them know you're one tough bitch (that the proper word for a female dog, so I'm not being off-color here). I would also suggest keeping a muzzle on hand for those times they really get out of control.

And for the darling little tail wagger, keep scratching their ears and rubbing their tummies, especially in front of the other dogs. Give them "treats" to eat and be sure they get the best toys to play with and always save a special bone for them. Just remember, all dogs really want to belong to the pack, but some of them just haven't had enough obedience training yet.

And now for the crabby 'bean counters.' This will be your greatest challenge. Health Care Reform has upset the whole hospital neighborhood. Everyone is prowling around trying to mark new territories to dominate. You could try leaving your scent on top of theirs to reclaim your turf, but I don't suggest that. Pretty soon the whole place will stink like an untended kennel. Instead, you must constantly keep your eye on these bad doggies. Notice when they begin to sniff around your unit, looking for a place to squirt and catch them before they start. Start barking and chase them away, snarl and growl if you have to, or better yet, get your whole pack of yippers, howlers and snarlers together and give the attack command. These snippy dogs don't belong in our clinical neighborhoods, so they must be chased away. Maybe someday we'll have an effective "Doggy Be Gone" spray that will discourage further intrusions.

As "Nancy Nurse," I became Patty's 'inner jester' after she'd been in nursing for fifteen years! By that time, she had "Been there, done that, got the T-shirt" if you know what I mean. It was time for her to carry the message she'd learned about humor and laughter to nurses and caregivers around the world. She was eager to do that, but didn't have the confidence that she could always see the funny side of every situation. I told her I'd ride along with her and offer all the crazy wisdom she needed."

Nurse Kindheart

"People need to know that someone cares about them, they need to be very certain of this. It is especially important when people are sick. It's important for the patient to feel cared for AND it's important for the caregiver to feel cared for. Too much time is spent these days using machines and drugs to combat illness. And that's just what it is, it's combat, it's a war against disease.

Unfortunately, the patient's poor body is the battlefield. We can no longer continue to drop these atomic bombs on the enemy just to prove that we're more powerful than the disease. We must learn to use our negotiation skills to impose economic sanctions, and avoid the blood shed if at all possible. Every soldier needs time away from the battlefield for Rest and Recovery. This is true for patients as well as professional and family caregivers. Everyone needs a safe space where they can relax and feel nurtured. So we must offer our caring with a kind heart, compassion and love. Love is the power that heals.

I decided to join up with Patty when she began speaking to patient support groups and doing hospital clown rounds. The outrageous, irreverent "Nancy Nurse" was just a bit too wild and bawdy for the fragile emotions of many sick people. When you're in the hospital or sick at home, you really want and need compassion and kindness. Someone to look out for you and protect you from insensitive people. Well, I fit that description to a 'T,' so I offered to travel around with Patty and help her out."

The Clown Prepares for Duty

I sit before the mirror, pasting this red nose on my face... It has become such a part of me, a nose I trust to help me open the door to that sick little boy's heart. I wonder if I will have the sensitivity and skill that is required to "be there" with his pain. I know the answers are all in my heart, but how do I keep my heart open in the face of his suffering? How can I keep it together and not become unglued? I need some wisdom greater than that inside of me. I know that I can be a channel, a vessel, an instrument of love and peace. I know that God will help me, if I only ask. But what does God know about clowning? And then I remember, this isn't about being a clown, it's about letting the love of God pour through me, while I'm dressed as a clown. The costume and make-up will get the little boy's attention, but the real healing power will come through my ability to love and accept, to forgive and surrender. I know I must Let Go and Let God. So I prepare with a prayer that has been repeated by clowns throughout time.

A Clown's Prayer

Lord, as I stumble through this life,
help me to create more laughter than tears,
dispense more happiness than gloom,
spread more cheer than despair.
Never let me become so indifferent that I will fail to see the
wonder in the eyes of a child or the twinkle in the
eyes of the aged.
Never let me forget that my total effort is to cheer people,
to make them happy and forget, at least for a moment, all
the unpleasant things in their lives.
And, Lord, in my final moment, may I hear You whisper,
"When you made My people smile, you made Me smile."

— Author Unknown

CHAPTER CHAT

NANCY NURSE: Well, after reading this chapter, I'm realizing that the "world's oldest profession" may not be what we thought it was all these years! Maybe clowning is older!

NURSE KINDHEART: You may be right. Fools, clowns, and jesters have certainly been an important part of almost every society since the beginning of time.

NANCY NURSE: I never knew there were so many different types of clowns or styles of clowning.

NURSE KINDHEART: Well dear, people are complex and history proves that societies and cultures will change over time. It's only natural to expect the function of the clown to change too.

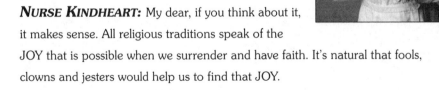

NANCY NURSE: Yeah, but I was really surprised to learn that clowns were involved in sacred rituals and church activities! Isn't that sacrilege or something?

NURSE KINDHEART: My dear, if you think about it, it makes sense. All religious traditions speak of the JOY that is possible when we surrender and have faith. It's natural that fools, clowns and jesters would help us to find that JOY.

NANCY NURSE: That's downright Ho Ho Holy!

Chapter 6
The Sacred Heart:
The Spirit of Laughter

*As one matures in spiritual life, one becomes more comfortable
with paradox, more appreciative of life's ambiguities. One develops a sense
of life's irony, metaphor, and humor and a capacity to embrace the whole,
with its beauty and outrageousness, in the graciousness of the heart.*
—Jack Kornfield

What is spiritual awareness, spiritual maturity, spiritual enlightenment? For
that matter, what is spirit? And, while we're on the topic, who is God and
where does God reside? These are questions philosophers, theologians, and
prophets have argued for years. I don't claim to have the answers, but I do
have a few more questions to add to the pot. Does the spirit of laughter bring
us to a deeper awareness of God? Can our sense of humor provide a path to
spiritual maturity? Is compassionate laughter a sign of spiritual enlightenment? Let's explore some possible answers.

*Humor can be found in Zen, in the Native American cultures,
in the Jewish and Hindu traditions ... and in many others.
In all of them, masters, holy fools, and sages are cherished
as inexhaustible sources of sanity, healing, and wholeness.
Their laughter, in the words of Yuan-Wo, is "like a cool,
refreshing breeze passing through the source of all things."*

— Lorraine Kisly

Spirit is difficult to define and impossible to measure. Yet, when a person radiates the essence of spirit, we recognize its qualities immediately. A person of great spirit is joyful, compassionate and serene. As our spiritual awareness matures, we acquire the ability to forgive, let go, and surrender. As these spiritual qualities and abilities grow stronger we are filled with hope, gratitude, and acceptance. A person with a strong spirit can transcend difficulties.

While the essence of spirit is similar in different cultures and religions, people call their God by various names: Goddess, Krishna, Allah, Brahman, the Tao, the Almighty, Higher Power, Great Spirit, or simply God. I like Larry Dossey's generic, politically correct, all inclusive label: the Absolute (Dossey, 1993).

Does God reside in the heavens above as Christians believe, or in the earth below as in many Native cultures, or is God the inner voice that Quakers listen for?

> *God is a sphere whose center is everywhere and whose circumference is nowhere.*
>
> *—Hermes Trismegistus*

Religion is not the same as spirit. Religions have been created to pass along the wisdom of spiritual teachers. They establish symbols and rituals to remind us of the Absolute. Religions help us to experience spirit and incorporate it into our lives. They provide a place where people can come together to explore and express their beliefs, attitudes and values. Religious traditions vary dramatically in their beliefs, practices and doctrines, but, the qualities of spirit are universal.

Conrad Hyers, Professor of Religious History, has dedicated his academic career to the study of humor and spirituality in Eastern and Western cultures. He has authored several books about this connection (Hyers, 1981; Hyers, Hyers, 1996). In a recent interview with the *Humor and Health Journal,* he clarifies the relationship between humor, religion and faith:

> "Consider the many debates throughout the history of the church over what is the meaning of being 'created in the image and likeness of God.' You find a tendency to deal with it as a very somber and

weighty manner. We congratulate ourselves on having reason, conscience, spirit, soul, etc.. attributes we might be willing to say have a certain godliness about them.

Rarely, do you ever find anyone suggesting that part of the 'image and likeness of God' is a sense of humor. Yet, when you think about it, seriousness is what we share with the animals. In laughter, we laugh alone. Laughter and sense of humor seem to be uniquely human. Approaching it from this angle, there are intimations of some important connections between humor and faith.

Those whose confidence rests in God and not in themselves are free to laugh and play in a way not available to others. People see religion as dealing with ultimate issues, which seem to require the ultimate in seriousness. This is a common bias against making a close connection between spirituality and humor or comedy. Ultra-seriousness really correlates with a lack of faith, or rather, it corresponds with faith in oneself as arbiter of some final knowledge of good and evil.

Ultra-serious, dogmatic persons are convinced that they are right, seemingly without qualification, and have the ultimate answers on the subject at hand. But that is not really faith in God, but rather faith in oneself and one's own capacities." (Dunn, 1996, pp 3-10.)

Laughter of a Spiritual Leader

The Dalai Lama is the spiritual leader of Tibet who has lived in exile in Dharamsala, India since the Chinese invaded Tibet in 1959. He radiates the spiritual qualities of joy, compassion and serenity. A friend of mine attended a talk by the Dalai Lama, who at one point began to laugh, a deep, easy, joyful laugh. As his laughter continued, she believed she could feel the depth of his spirit. Despite living in exile, he is still able to let go of his hatred and find serenity. In 1989 when he received the Nobel Peace prize, he was asked by a reporter, "Your Holiness, how can you feel compassion for the Chinese after all they have done?" The Dalai Lama replied, "They have taken everything from us. Should I let them take my mind as well? We must let go of our resentment, anger and hatred to find compassion, and compassion is the key to happiness" (Goleman, 1992).

If you want others to be happy, practice compassion.
If you want to be happy, practice compassion.

— Dalai Lama

Laughter and Letting Go

Humor helps us let go of our restricted view of a situation. We detach from our problems and gain new and expanded perspectives. We let go of uncomfortable, unhealthy emotions when we laugh. The cathartic cleansing of a good laugh washes away our anger, anxiety and animosity.

Illness gives us plenty to feel anxious and angry about, but a good dose of humor can help us cope with those emotions. Erma Bombeck spent one summer at a cancer camp for children and wrote a funny and poignant book about how kids use their sense of humor to cope with their illness, hair loss, and chemotherapy. She writes, "Kids get pretty creative with their answers when someone asks what happened to their hair" (Bombeck, 1989). These are a few of their hilarious responses:

> I got sick of getting shampoo in my eyes.
> The wind just blew it out.
> My father is Kojak.
> I just joined the Marines.

> *Erma couldn't resist adding some of her own:*
> I sold it.
> Bad genes. My mother is bald.
> You'll never guess why I just fired my hairdresser.
> I traded it for this body.

Spirit of Innocence and Play

Keep away from the wisdom that does not cry,
the philosophy that does not laugh, and the greatness
that does not bow before children.

—Kahil Gibran

Many religions talk of the importance of a childlike innocence, the ability to meet each new moment with a sense of awe and wonder. In Zen Buddhism, this is called "beginner's mind," an ability to see with the freshness and immediacy of the little child, full of amazement and wonder. When the disciples asked Jesus about how they could be assured of entry into heaven, he advised, "Truly, I say to you, unless you turn and become like children, you will never enter the kingdom of heaven. Whoever humbles himself like this child, he is the greatest in the kingdom of heaven" (Matthew 18: 2-4).

In China during the eighth century, Ho-tai, the Laughing Buddha, was a model for spiritual practice. This jolly, rotund, pot-bellied Zen monk was supposedly modeled after an actual wandering Chinese monk named Keishi. Paintings from this era show Ho-tai dancing merrily in the streets with children. With a big silly grin across his broad face and a large linen sack containing all his worldly possessions slung over his shoulder, Ho-tai looks like a playful overgrown child. He refuses to remain inside the cloistered walls and maintain a strict monastic discipline. Instead, his entire religious practice consists of playing with the village children. Ho-tai's message is that you can be enlightened and still have a belly laugh. He is a playful, joyous fat man, who drinks a little wine, and would rather play hide and seek with children all day than chant sutras with a bunch of old monks in a stifling hot temple. He believed that children knew what monks did not, that the presence of God could be felt in every moment if we remain playful (Nisker, 1990).

Laughter of Children

Children experience laughter in response to any pleasant surprise. I remember a day when my son, Ken was about 9 months-old. It was warm and sunny, so I placed his playpen on the lawn outside my apartment door. He was playing happily with his toys, when I went upstairs to borrow a tool from a neighbor. As we watched him play from the balcony, my neighbor and I made a paper airplane and flew it down to him. As the toy airplane drifted and looped its way down, my son watched, intently at first. Then he giggled and finally he burst into peels of robust laughter. We were immediately caught up in his joy and delight and we quickly began launching more and more airplanes just to hear him laugh. His laughter flowed like a well-spring and quenched our thirsty hearts that were dry from the seriousness and solemnity of adult life and responsibilities.

The laughter of the innocent child is exuberant and finds joy in each moment. The humor of a child plays with life, is surprised by life, and delights in life. Children frolic, act silly and play with fearless abandon. There are no rules, plans, or goals. They simply enjoy playing for the sake of playing. During these moments, they surrender into the present and accept whatever the next moment may bring.

> *To be playful is not to be trivial or frivolous or act*
> *as though nothing of consequence will happen.*
> *On the contrary, when we are playful with each other,*
> *we relate as free persons, and the relationship is open*
> *to surprise; everything that happens is of consequence,*
> *for seriousness is a dread of the unpredictable.*
> *To be serious is to press for a specified conclusion.*
> *To be playful is to allow for unlimited possibility.*
>
> *—James Carse*

Humor of the Innocent Child

A few years ago, in a hospital near San Diego, a nurse gave me a copy of an essay one of her Sunday School students had written. It is a wonderful example of the humor which can arise when children innocently combine the facts they know with a bit of imagination. Thank you Danny, for your wonderful, innocent understanding.

An Essay On God

"One of God's main jobs is making people. He makes these to put in place of the ones that die, so there will be enough people to take care of things here on earth. God's second most important job is listening to prayers. An awful lot of this goes on, as some people, like preachers, pray other times besides bedtime. God doesn't have time to listen to the radio or TV on account of this. God sees everything and hears everything and is everywhere. Which keeps Him pretty busy.

Jesus is God's Son. He used to do all the hard work, like walking on water and doing miracles and trying to teach people about God who didn't want to learn. They finally got tired of His preaching to them and they crucified Him. God appreciated everything He had done and all His hard work on earth so God told Him He didn't have to go out on the road any more. Now he helps His Father out by listening to prayers and seeing which things are important for God to take care of and which ones He can take care of Himself without having to bother God. Like a secretary only more important, of course. You can pray anytime you want and they are sure to hear you because they've got it worked out so one of them is on duty all the time. And that's why I believe in God."

—Danny Dutton, age 8

Comedians Acting Like Kids

My favorite comedian is Lily Tomlin. She is a master of capturing a character and portraying it so convincingly that she doesn't need costumes or props.

During the 1970's, Tomlin performed on the television show, *Saturday Night Live*. My favorite character from that show was Edith Ann. Edith is about 5 years-old and usually begins each sketch sitting in a huge wooden chair. The chair is so large, that Tomlin's adult body actually looks like a small child in a big chair. When Edith speaks, you are certain that she has a severely stuffed up nose as she shares her wise thoughts and observations with the audience. At the end of the sketch, she always concluded with, "And that's the truth." Listen, while she shares her truth about God (Wagner, 1994).

> *Sometimes I think it is like this:*
> *God has a TV set*
> *and God watches us on it.*
> *Whenever I think I'm being watched,*
> *I always sing and dance*
> *and do a commercial for myself.*
>
> — *"Edith Ann" written by Jane Wagner*

Even the most scholarly theologian would have difficulty arguing with her innocent logic. And if she were right, how many of us would do exactly as she advises? And that's the truth!

Belonging and Connectedness

People describe spirit as a deep sense of connection to all things, an awareness that they are not separate from God, but that God lives inside of them. This connection to the whole of life, removes feelings of separation and loneliness and provides a sense of belonging to something much greater than our small individual existence. We begin to feel secure, peaceful and serene. Because we are safe, we can be open with compassion and acceptance of every thing in every moment.

Q: What did the Buddhist say to the hot dog vendor?
A: Please, make me one with everything.

Humor and Connectedness

Humor connects people and brings them together. Before we can laugh at the humor, we must "get the gag" or "identify with" the struggles and courage of the clown. Only then can we begin to laugh. When we laugh together, and share our mutual amusement and joy, we feel bonded with our "joy mates" and begin to relax, trust and open up. Sharing a comedic moment with others increases our own enjoyment. Have you ever noticed how much deeper you laugh when you see a movie or humorous routine with another person? The closer you felt to that person before the comedy, the deeper your laughter will be, during the comedy. Laughing together with family and friends, is more satisfying than laughing with strangers. Humor creates connections between the body, the mind, and the spirit. As we learned in Chapter Three, psycho-neuroimmunology measures the power and intricacy of these connections. Humor, when used with compassion, will increase our sense of connection with others, and with life itself. As we connect in laughter, we experience an awareness of life and each other that extends far beyond our individual existence. This connection and awareness is the essence of any spiritual practice.

Some styles of humor do not stimulate compassionate laughter. When humor is caustic, judgmental or offensive, it lacks harmony and attunement. We withdraw, close down and protect ourselves from humor that bites. Observe the type of humor people choose to use. Does it express compassion and create connections, or does it show hostility and produce defensiveness? Practice humor that is 'gummy'—soft, with no teeth!

Adolescent Humor - Awkwardness and Tension

Our sense of humor matures right along with our physical and psychological development. Humor is not all innocence and play. As we grow beyond childhood, we become more aware of the anxieties, doubts, conflicts, and the ambiguities of our existence. As adolescents, we become aware of our sexuality, nakedness, and awkwardness. Our humor style shifts and changes during this time to allow for a venting of those fears, tensions and conflicts. Jokes focus on sex, food, and body waste, or on people in society that threaten us, like teachers and parents. Because adolescents feel insecure, they use humor to protect themselves and feel superior. *Mad* magazine, full of satire and outrageous parodies, has always been popular with adolescents. The movie, *Wayne's World,* was a big hit. It captured the creative rebellion of most teens as Garth and his friend planned sexual escapades with the "babes," and the dialogue captured the amusing style and colloquialisms of "teen-speak."

> *The more one suffers, the more, I believe, one has*
> *a sense of the comic. It is only by the deepest suffering*
> *that one acquires the authority in the art of the comic.*
>
> *—Soren Kiekegaard*

If teenagers kept all the emotions of puberty inside of them they might become violent, get depressed or withdraw completely from life. The release of tension through caustic humor about frightening subjects is a way for teenagers to stay balanced and healthy. Many popular comedians, like Andrew Dice Clay, build entire routines around hateful feelings. He is so bad, I'm not even going to give you an example of his racist, sexist, agist, homophobic remarks. Many adolescents enjoy this type of material as a safe way to ventilate feelings and find humor in their 'oppression.' The trick is not to get stuck in the stage of adolescent humor.

Mature Humor - Compassion and Serenity

After emerging successfully from the doubt, anxiety and conflict of adolescence, we gain a sense of resolution and come to terms with who we are. A recent study measured children's laughter at a frequency of 400 times per day while adults averaged about twenty-five times per day. (And we all know some adults for whom even that number would be a challenge). Somewhere between childhood and adulthood, we sober up. At this point our humor changes. It no longer judges others, but rather expresses love, compassion and mercy. We no longer laugh at others, but rather, accept others in spite of our differences.

The humor of maturity is the ability to laugh at others and ourselves, as we all share common predicaments, embarrassments and temptations. Mature humor returns to the lighthearted playfulness of the child, but is no longer the playfulness of innocence. Rather, it is the playfulness of one who has experienced suffering, but has not been conquered by it. We are able to laugh, be playful and lighthearted, in spite of, and in a sense because of, the conflicts and disappointments of life. Adult humor emerges from a sense of harmony, peace, and liberation, and it is used to express our faith, love, hope and compassion. It is at this stage that we find Compassionate Laughter (Hyers, 1996).

Beyond jokes and even words, the laughing spirit is the essence of natural mirth that connects all human hearts in an unspoken universal language of gentle delight. Humor of the laughing spirit includes all human beings, is never at the expense of an individual or group, and does not depend on cleverness or wit to be understood. The pleasant release of tension, the relief that causes us to smile or chuckle when we feel the presence of the laughing spirit, comes from the sudden realization that we are not separate from each other after all.

—Lee Glickstein

Ah, Sweet Mystery of Life

Life is a mystery. Why do some people get sick? It doesn't make sense. They are non-smoking, exercising, meditating, vegetarians. It's not fair. It's a mystery. Great spiritual leaders, saints and mystics often die from illnesses that bring severe pain and great suffering. Saint Bernadette, who saw the vision of the Virgin at Lourdes, where thousands of healings have since occurred, died of tuberculosis at the age of thirty-five. The famous spiritual teacher Krishnamurti, died of cancer of the pancreas. Suzuki Roshi, who brought Zen Buddhism from Japan to the United States, died of liver cancer. The most beloved saint of modern India, Sri Ramana Maharshi, died of stomach cancer (Dossey, 1993).

Why? Why did these holy people die? They prayed, meditated and served God. How could this happen? It's a mystery. Most of us know, or have at least heard of, someone who lives a wild and unhealthy life. They smoke and drink to excess, eat foods full of salt and fat, and never exercise. Yet, these people live to be 80 years-old without any serious illness. It doesn't make sense. It's a mystery.

There is no answer.
There never has been an answer.
There never will be an answer.
And that's the answer.

—Gertrude Stein

Life presents many unanswered questions. We can agonize over the why's, or struggle with the how's, and still, we may never understand the answer. Spiritual maturity presents a third choice. Simply accept life on its own terms. Accept without controlling. Let go. Accept without questioning. Surrender. Accept without bitterness. Forgive. God will reward you. You will be filled with joy, compassion and serenity.

My life is but a weaving between my Lord and me,
I cannot chose the colors, He weaveth steadily.
Sometimes He weaveth sorrow, and I in foolish pride,
Forget He sees the upper and I the underside.
Not 'til the loom is silent and the shuttles cease to fly,
Shall God unroll the canvas and explain the reason why.
The dark threads are as needful in the weaver's skillful hands,
As the ones of gold and silver in the path that He has planned.

—Author Unknown

Compassionate laughter will help you let go, teach you to surrender, and encourage you to forgive. As your humor develops from innocence and play, through tension and conflict, and finally, to compassion and peace, you will find a greater awareness of God.

CHAPTER CHAT

NANCY NURSE: What else can I say?

NURSE KINDHEART:
AMEN!

Epilogue

Imagine. The year is 2010 and therapeutic humor is now accepted as a complementary treatment in health care. Today you have an appointment to see your physician because of a persistent headache. The appointment is conveniently scheduled after working hours. You arrive at the doctor's office, tired from the day's work and anxious about the possible cause of your headache. After all, your father had a brain tumor removed when he was about your age. As you enter the office, the receptionist smiles and welcomes you. He offers you a small tape player with headphones and a choice of comedy audio cassettes to entertain you while you wait. You choose your favorite comedian and settle back. Your anxiety and fatigue begin to melt, and you begin to relax. Soon you are laughing!

You are called into the examination room, where a bulletin board of cartoons keeps you amused until the physician arrives. In a few moments, the doctor enters the room. You talk about your families and your latest vacation adventures. She offers to share a few new jokes, and soon you are both laughing together. You relax a bit more and a sense of connection and trust begins to build between you. After a thorough examination, she explains some concerns she has and requests that you complete a CAT scan before the end of the week.

Later that week, you arrive at the hospital and register with the clerk at the Outpatient Clinic. As you sit across her desk and she types information into the computer, you notice a box with a few toys. She invites you to play with them while she prepares your chart. Soon you have several wind-up toys moving and hopping around the desk top! You are both smiling as she hands you the chart and directs you to the Radiology Department.

You take the elevator to the basement and enter the crowded waiting room. It is obvious that this room is shared by those awaiting radiation therapy appointments, as well as those scheduled for diagnostic procedures. Some small children who appear to be quite ill, are sitting near their worried parents. Suddenly, you hear music, a perky little tune created by an ukulele and a penny whistle. Everyone turns towards the music and starts to smile as two clowns enter the waiting room. They move about greeting people, introducing their puppets and blowing bubbles which the children try to catch on their noses. Some people receive a "clown nose transplant," others receive colorful stickers. After ten minutes, almost everyone in the room is laughing. Some are amused by the comical antics of the clowns, others comforted by the delight shining from the eyes of these sick children.

After your CAT scan and subsequent angiogram are determined to be normal, your physician concludes that your headaches are most likely caused by the unrelieved tension, pressures and deadlines at your workplace. She asks that you meet with her office nurse for some stress management training. You expect to be given the same information about relaxation, exercise, and diet that you've heard before, but this time is different. Your nurse talks about the health benefits of humor and laughter. After answering many questions about your preference for humor styles and artists, he creates a list of humorous books, audio and video tapes and articles about humor, all available from the Laughter Library at the hospital or the humor section of the local community library. You receive a list of humorous videotapes for rent at a local video outlet, as well as a list of nearby comedy clubs and their phone numbers. You remember how relaxed you felt each time you laughed through the tensions of the last week, how the comedy tapes, cartoons, toys and clowns all brought welcome relief from the stress of the moment.

You make a promise to yourself: a promise to protect your health and well being by seeking and responding to moments of humor and laughter—*JEST FOR YOUR HEALTH!*

Glossary of Terms

The following definitions are provided for the reader who wishes to understand the highly technical language of the current immunological literature and the research studies we have referenced in this book. An excellent scientific discussion of the immune system, it's structure, function and interactions is provided in the book, *Immunology,* by Janis Kuby, Professor of Biology at San Francisco State University (Kuby, 1994).

Antibody: A protein (immunoglobulin) that recognizes a particular portion of an antigen and facilitates the effectiveness of the cell mediated response. B cells that have not encountered antigen express membrane-bound antibody. Plasma cells produce antibodies that are secreted into the serum and lymph.

Antigen: Any substance that binds specifically to an antibody or a T-cell receptor.

Antigen-presenting cell (APC): Macrophages, B cells and other cells that can process and present antigenic peptides.

Autoimmunity: An abnormal immune response against self-antigens.

B cell: A lymphocyte that matures in the bone marrow and expresses membrane-bound antibody. Following interaction with antigen, it differentiates into antibody-secreting plasma cells and memory cells.

CD3: A polypeptide complex associated with the t-cell receptor and functions in signal transduction.

CD4: A membrane molecule found on those T cells that recognize antigenic peptides associated with a class II MHC molecule.

CD8: A membrane molecule found on those T cells (usually cytotoxic T cells) that recognize antigenic peptides associated with a class I MHC molecule.

Cell-mediated immunity: Host defenses that are mediated by antigen-specific T cells and various nonspecific cells of the immune system. It protects against intracellular bacteria, viruses and cancer and is responsible for graft rejection. Transfer of primed T cells confers this type of immunity on the recipient.

Chemotaxis: Directional movement of cells in response to the concentration gradient of some substance.

Cortisol: One of the corticosteroids that promotes the formation of carbohydrates, alters connective tissue response to injury, and is an anti-inflammatory agent.

Cytokine: Any of numerous secreted, proteins that regulate the intensity and duration of the immune response by exerting a variety of effects on lymphcytes and other immune cells.

Effector cell: Any cell capable of mediating an immune function (e.g. activated helper T, cells, cytotoxic T lymphocyte and plasma cells).

Fc receptor: Cell-surface receptor specific for the Fc portion of certain classes of immunoglobulin. It is present on lymphocytes, mast cells, macrophages, and other accessory cells.

Humoral immunity: Host defenses that are mediated by antibody present in the plasma, lymph, and tissue fluids. It protects against extracellular bacteria and foreign macromolecules. Transfer of antibodies confers this type of immunity on the recipient.

Interferon: Several glycoproteins produced and secreted by certain cells that induce an antiviral state in other cells and also help to regulate the immune response. Alpha-interferon and Beta interferon primarily provide antiviral protection, whereas Gamma interferon which is produced by T cells, has numerous effects on various immune-system cells.

Interleukin: A group of cytokines secreted by leukocytes that primarily affect the growth and differentiation of various hematopoietic and immune-system cells.

Leukocyte: Any blood cell that is not an erythrocyte; commonly refered to as a white blood cell.

Ligand: Any molecule recognized by a receptor.

Lymph: A pale, watery, proteinaceous fluid that is derived from intercellular tissue fluid and circulates in lymphatic vessels.

Lymph node: A small secondary lymphoid organ that contains lymphocytes, macrophages, and dendritic cells and serves as a site for filtration of foreign antigen and activation and proliferation of lymphocytes.

Lymphocyte: A mononuclear leukocyte that mediates humoral or cell mediated immunity.

Lymphokine: A cytokine produced by activated lymphocytes, especially T-helper cells.

Lysosome: A small cytoplasmic vesicle found in many types of cells that contains hydrolytic enzymes, which play an important role in the digestion of material ingested by phagocytosis and endocytosis.

Macrophage: A large, myeloid cell derived from a monocyte that functions in phagocytosis, antigen processing and presentation, secretion of cytokines, and antibody dependent cell-mediated cytotoxicity.

Memory cell: Clonally expanded progeny of T and B cells formed during the primary response following initial exposure to an antigen. Memory cells are more easily activated than naive lymphocytes and when they encounter antigen in a subsequent exposure, they mediate a faster and greater secondary response.

MHC - Major Histocompatibility Complex: A complex of genes encoding cell surface molecules that are required for antigen presentation to T cells and for rapid graft rejection.

Monocyte: A mononuclear, phagocytic myeloid cell that circulates briefly in the bloodstream before migrating into the tissues where it becomes a macrophage.

Natural killer cell (NK): A large, granular lymphocyte (null cell) that has cytotoxic ability but does not express antigen-binding receptors. It is an antibody-independent killer of tumor cells and also can participate in antibody-dependent cell-mediated cytotoxicity.

Neurohormones: Hormones that either stimulate or are made by the nerves and the nervous system. Many are released into the system as the result of stress.

Neurotransmitter: A chemical that is discharged from a nerve-fiber ending to carry messages that bring about direct changes in the body's systems.

Neuropeptide: A neurotransmitter made up of amino acids that is active in the brain or nervous system. Endorphins and enkephalins are neuropeptides.

Phagocytosis: A process by which certain cells (phagocytes) engulf microorganisms, other cells and foreign particles.

Plasma cell: A differentiated, antibody-secreting cell derived from an antigen-activated B cell.

Primary lymphoid organ: An organ in which lymphocyte precursors mature into immunocompetent cells. In mammals, the bone marrow and thymus gland are the primary lymphoid organs in which B-cell and T-cell maturation occurs, respectively.

Receptor: Cell-surface molecule present on the cell membrane that has high affinity for a particular ligand. Lymphocytes have receptors for both antigens and neurohormones. Nerve cells only have receptors for neurotransmitters, not antigens.

Sensitized lymphocytes: Effector T cells derived from exposure of naive T cells to antigen; on subsequent exposure to the same antigen, they rapidly carry out their effector functions.

Specificity: Antigenic capacity of antibody and T-cell receptor to recognize and interact with a single, unique antigenic determinant.

Spleen: Secondary lymphoid organ where old erythrocytes are destroyed and blood-borne antigens are trapped and presented to lymphocytes.

Suppressor T-Cell: Inhibit the generation or progression of immune responses to specific antigens.

T cell: A lymphocyte that matures in the thymus and expresses a T-cell recptor, CD3 and CD4 or CD8. Several distinct T-cell subpopulations are recognized.

T cytotoxic cell: Generally a CD8+, class I MHC-restricted T cell, which differentiates into a cytotoxic T lymphocyte following interaction with altered self-cells (e.g. tumor cells, virus-infected cells).

T helper cell: Generally a CD4+ class II MHC-restricted T cell, which plays a central role in both humoral and cell-mediated immunity and secretes numerous cytokines when activated.

Thymus: A primary lymphoid organ, located in the thoracic cavity, where T-cell maturation occurs.

Tumor necrosis factors (TNF): Two related cytokines produced by macrophages (TNF-alpha) and some T cells (TNF-beta). Both factors are cytotoxic to tumor cells but not to normal cells.

Vaccination: Intentional administration of a harmless or less harmful form of a pathogen to induce a specific immune response that protects the individual against later expsure to the same pathogen.

Humor Resource List

Humor Associations

American Association for Therapeutic Humor

Networking and educational opportunities for helping professionals who are interested in healing humor. Excellent bi-monthly newsletter, *Therapeutic Humor,* provides the latest information as well as practical suggestions for humor programs.
222 S. Meramec, Ste. 303
St. Louis, MO 63105
Phone: (314) 863-6232, Fax: (314) 863-6457

International Society for Humor Studies

Organization for academic researchers from the disiplines of English, Psychology, Sociology, Literature, History, Physiology, Medicine and Nursing. Quarterly journal of research findings, and an Annual International Conference.
Don Nilsen, Ph.D., Secretary
Arizona State University, Dept. of English
Tempe, AZ 85287-0302
Phone: (602) 965-7592, Fax: (602) 965-3451
Email: atdfn@asuvm.inre.asu.edu

Christian Humor

Clown Ministry

Active ministry program in the community and prisons.
Don Berkoski
4149 Golden Eagle Dr.
Indianapolis, IN 46234

Clown Ministry Cooperative

Provides training programs in clown ministry.
Phoenix Power and Light, Inc.
PO Box 820
Oxon Hill, MD 20745

Clown Ministry Supplies

Props and magic tricks with a Christian message.

Dewey's Good News

1202 Wildwood Dr.

Deer Park, TX 77536

Fellowship of Merry Christians, Inc.

Excellent interdenominational resource for church pastors, Sunday School teachers—anyone interested in the power and importance of humor in Christian practice.

PO Box 668

Kalamazoo, MI 49005-0668

Phone: (800) 877-2757

Four Heaven's Sake!

Religious Barbershop Quartet.

Lou Sutcliffe

1222 S. Loara St., #14

Anaheim, CA 92802

Phone: (714) 774-2232

Humor Publications

A Chance to Cut is a Chance to Cure

Booklet of funny comments made by medical interns and residents. To order, send check for $5.00 to: Rip Pfeiffer, MD; 171 Louiselle St., Mobile AL 36607

Clown Alley

Official bi-monthly publication of the International Shrine Clown Association.

ISCA, PO Box 878-L, Safety Harbor, FL 34695

Funny Times

Monthly newpaper of the best cartoons and humorous articles gathered from publications around the United States.

PO Box 18530, Cleveland Heights, OH 44118; Phone: (216) 371-8600

Humor and Health Journal

Excellent bi-monthly journal. Features interviews with prominent humor researchers as well as a review of humorous books and the latest humor research.
PO Box 16814, Jackson, MS 39236; Phone and Fax: (601) 957-0075

Journal of Nursing Jocularity

Excellent source of nursing humor featuring funny stories, jokes and cartoons. Publishes a catalog of humorous books, tapes and toys relating to humor in nursing; sponsor of the annual Humor Skills conference.
PO Box 40416, Mesa, AZ 85274; Phone: (602) 835-6165, Fax: (602) 835-6922
Email: laffinrn@neta.com

Laughing Matters

Wonderful quarterly publication from The Humor Project. Loaded with practical advice about how to increase humor in our life and work. Publishes a large catalog of humorous books and tapes for a diverse audience; sponsor of the Annual Humor and Creativity Conference.
110 Spring St., Saratoga Springs, NY 12866; Phone: (518) 587-8770

LaughMakers Magazine

Excellent resource for clowns, magicians, story tellers, puppeteers and others interested in adding more humor and laughter to their performances.
PO Box 160, Syracuse, NY 13215; Phone: (314) 492-4523
E-mail: lafmaker@aol.com

Laughter Prescription Newsletter

Bi-monthly newsletter filled with articles, interviews, advice and ideas for bringing laughter into your life.
7720 El Camino Real, # B225, Carlsbad, CA 92009; Phone: (800) 794-8667
Fax: (619) 634-1405, Email: klee@connectnet.com

Stitches—Journal of Medical Humor

Bi-monthly journal for and by physicians about the humorous aspects of medicine and clinical practice.
14845 Yonge St., #300, Aurora, Ontario Canada L4G 6H8; Phone: (800) 668-7412

Clown Resources

Archie McPhee and Company
Catalog of humorous toys and props.
PO Box 30852, Seattle, WA 98103; Phone: (206) 745-0711
Email: mcphee@halcyon.com

Big Apple Circus - Clown Care Unit
Largest organized hospital clown program in the USA.
35 West 35th St., 9th Floor, New York, NY 10001; Phone: (212) 268-2500

Cherri-Oats and Co.
Catalog of clown supplies, makeup, wigs, etc.
PO Box 723, N. Olmsted, OH 44070; Phone: (216) 979-9971

Clowns of America International
Professional and amateur clown organization supporting the practice of clown-ing. Annual conference, local chapters and bi-monthly magazine for members with helpful advice and announcements.
PO Box 570, Lake Jackson, TX 77566-0570

Clown Camp, Richard Snowberg, Director
Excellent training for the novice and experienced clown. Special focus on "Caring Clown" or "Clown Ministry" training. Week-long residential trainings in June and weekend trainings sponsored in a variety of cities around the USA.
University of Wisconsin at LaCrosse, 1725 State St., LaCrosse, WI 54601
Phone: (608) 785-6505

Clown Shoes
12 Orlando St., Springfield, MA 01108

Clown Supplies
Excellent catalog with a wide variety of clown props, books, make-up and magic tricks.
The Castles, Tre. 101, Ste. C-7C, Brentwood, NH 03833
Phone and Fax: (603) 679-3311

Clown Training with Master Clown Frosty Little
Advanced training for clowns from a Master Ringling Bros. circus clown with 25 years of performing experience.
222 E. 8th St., Burley, ID 83318; Phone: (208) 678-0005

Comanche Clown Shoes
PO Box 551, Mountain View, OK 73062; Phone: (800) 832-3424; (405) 347-2817

Costumes by Betty
2181 Edgerton St., St. Paul, MI 55117; Phone: (612) 771-8734, (813) 948-0206

Costumes by Pricilla Mooseburger
PO Box 700, Maple Lake, MN 55358; Phone: (612) 963-6277

Designers of Smiles
Catalog of clown supplies.
4125 Stagwood Dr., Raleigh, NC 27613; Phone: (919) 282-8841

Freckles Clown Supplies
Catalog of clown supplies.
5509 Roosevelt Blvd., Jacksonville, FL 32244
Phone: (904) 388-5541, Fax: (904) 388-5556

Fun Technicians
Wonderful resource for props and tricks for clown magic routines.
PO Box 160, Syracuse, NY 13215; Phone: (315) 492-4523, Fax: (315) 469-1392

Heart-to-Heart Hospital Clown Newsletter
5835 Marshall St., Oakland, CA 94608

Hospital Clowning Video
A how-to video about incorporating clowning into hospital visits.
PO Box 2939, Orange Park, FL 32067; Phone: (904) 272-5878

LaRock's Fun and Magic Outlet
Source for a variety of magic tricks.
3847 Rosehaven, Charlotte, NC 28205; Phone: (800) 473-3425

Rubber Chicken Gags
Rubber chickens and a booklet of funny routines.
34 Harris Ct., Cheektowaga, NY 14225

San Francisco Clown School, Arina Isaacson
Excellent clown training with an emphasis on character development. Weekend
intensive programs available.
1000 Prague, San Francisco, CA; Phone: (415) 587-3301

Slapstick Productions, Kenny Ahern
One of the best performing clowns in the United States.
2111 So. 15th Place, LaCrosse, WI 54601; Phone: (608) 787-0056

World Clown Association
Clowns from around the world promoting the growth and quality of clown practice. Quarterly journal with membership.
418 South Sixth St., Pekin, IL 61554; Phone and Fax: (309) 346-7093

Toys and Props

Anatomical Chart Company
Great source for funny props and novelties with an anatomical focus.
8221 N. Kimball, Skokie, IL 60076; Phone: (800) 621-7500

Ashleigh Brilliant, Pot Shots and Books
Books and postcards with amusing one liners and sketches.
117 West Valerio St., Santa Barbara, CA 93101; Phone: (800) 237-6053

Hair by Chemo
T-shirts and hats for cancer patients.
PO Box 216, Wauzeka, WI 53826; Phone: (800) 729-9713

In Your Face Cards, Brian Moench, MD
Funny greeting cards, calendars and T-shirts about health and medical care.
4091 Splendor Way, Salt Lake City, UT 84124; Phone: (800) 377-8878

Land of Mirth and Funny
Good source for funny buttons and other humorous props.
PO Box 50312, Irvine, CA 92619-0312; Phone: (714) 559-8148

Oriental Trading Company
Bulk purchase of novelty items.
PO Box 3407, Omaha, NE 68103-0407; Phone: (800) 228-2269

Peachey Keene Props
Hand sculpted foam props for clowns, ie: syringes, cameras, binoculars.
PO Box 147, Beallsville, PA 15313; Phone: (412) 769-5447

United Ad Label Co., Inc.
Excellent source for colorful and funny stickers, many with health themes. Ask for novelty catalogue.
PO Box 2216, Brea, CA 92622; Phone: (800) 423-4643

Wellness Quest Books
Publisher for Health Caretoons - book and calendar with cartoons.
1541 71/2 Ave. N.E., Rochester, MN 55906; Phone: (507) 281-3143

Audio and Video Tapes

Chordiac Arrest
Funny songs about medicine and health.
Barbershop Physicians, 527 East Third St., Lockport, IL 60441

Critics Choice Video
Catalog of a variety of videos, large comedy section.
PO Box 749, Itasca, IL 60143; Phone: (800) 367-7765

Life and Depth: Very Funny Stories About Very Scary Things, by Joe Kogel.
Cancer survivor talks about use of humor for his recovery.
50 Summit Ave., Providence, RI 02906; Phone: (401) 351-0229

Nursing Notes, Barbershop Quartet of Nurses
Funny songs about nursing and other topics.
Larry Brennan, RN, 253 Winthrop Rd., Syracuse, NY 13206; Phone: (315) 463-8971

Peter Alsop's Uplifting Children's Music, Moose School Productions
Special tape with songs about kids in hospitals.
PO Box 960, Topanga, CA 90290; Phone: (800) 676-5480

Postings Video Catalog
Catalog of a variety of videos, large comedy section.
PO Box 8001, Hilliard, OH 43026-8001; Phone: (800) 262-6604

Robo the Clown Series - CHTV at Children's Hospital
Video tape series to help children prepare for hospital procedures.
CH 242-840 Sherbrook Street, Winnipeg, Manitoba, Canada R2A 1S10

The Mind's Eye Audio and Video
Catalog of a variety of videos, large comedy section.
PO Box 1060, Petaluma, CA 94953; Phone: (800) 949-3333

Time Warner Viewer's Edge
Catalog of a variety of videos, large comedy section.
PO Box 3925, Milford, CT 06460; Phone: (800) 228-5440

Too Live Nurse
Funny songs about nursing reality, cardiac arrhythmias and pharmacology
PO Box 201, Canaan, NY 12029; Phone: (518) 781-4943.

Video Naturals Co.
Catalog for videos of ocean tides, forest streams, and more.
2590 Glen Green, Los Angeles, CA 90068; Phone: (213) 469-0019

Wolfe Video
Source for Lily Tomlin videos including her one woman show, *Search for Signs of Intelligent Life.*
PO Box 64, New Almaden, CA 95042; Phone: (408) 268-6782

World Wide Web Sites for Humor

Use search engine http://www.yahoo.com
Choose category Therapeutic Humor
American Association for Therapeutic Humor
http://www.callamer.com/itc/aath
In Your Face Cards
http://www.inyourface.com
Jest for the Health of It
http://www.mother.com/JestHome/
Journal of Nursing Jocularity
http://www.jocularity.com
Laugh Web
http://www.misty.com/laughweb/

Appendix

These are some of my favorite books and videotapes. They are available at your local bookstore, video stores, and some are available through the Humor catalogs listed in the Humor Resource guide. Enjoy!

Suggested Books for the Laughter Library:

The Patient's Experience

Babies and Other Hazards of Sex, by Dave Barry.

I Want to Grow Up, I Want to Grow Hair, I Want to Go to Boise, by Erma Bombeck, 1989.

And How Are We Feeling Today?, by Kathyrn Hammer, 1993.

Hormones from Hell, by Jan King, 1990.

It's Always Something, by Gilda Radner, 1989.

The Jester Has Lost His Jingle, by David Saltzman, 1995.

You're Only Old Once!, by Dr. Seuss, 1986.

The Health Professional's Experience

Best of Stitches, by Joe Cocker, 1992.

Journal of Nursing Jocularity: Catalog of Books and Tapes

Whinnoreha and Other Nursing Diagnosis, edited by Fran London, 1995.

A Chance to Cut is a Chance to Cure, by Rip Pfeiffer, 1985.

Cartoon Books

Build a Better Life by Stealing Office Supplies—Dilbert, by Scott Adams, 1995.

Medicine's the Best Laughter, by Gideon Bosker, 1995.

Garfield Treasury, by Jim Davis.

Health Care-toons, by Ed Fischer and Jeff Haebig, 1993.

Patients at Large, by Tom Jackson, 1990.

Classic Droodles, by Richard Price, 1992.

Herman Treasury, Vols. 1-8 (1979-1989), by Jim Unger.

Farcus, You're a Bum, by David Waisglass, 1993.

Tales from the Bedside, by John Wise, Available from J. of Nursing Jocularity.

Quick Reading Zingers

The 77 Habits of Highly Ineffective People, by Jim Becker et. al., 1994.

I Want to Reach Your Mind - Where is It Currently Located?, by Ashley Brilliant, 1994.

Murphy's Law, Book 1 & 2, by Arthur Bloch.

You're Not a Kid Anymore.... by Jeff Foxworthy, 1993.

I Am My Own Best Casual Acquaintance, by Shanti Goldstein, 1993.

Life is Like a Dogsled Team - Wit and Wisdom of Grizzard, by Lewis Grizzard, 1995.

Children's Letters to God, by Stuart Hample and Eric Marshall, 1991.

Quotations to Cheer You Up When the World is Getting You Down, by Allen Klein, 1991.

Anguished English, by Richard Lederer,1987.

Kids are Still Saying the Darndest Things, by Dandi Mackall, 1994.

Death Is - A Lighter Look at a Grave Situation, by Steve Mickle and Rich Hillman, 1993.

Codependent for Sure, by Jan Mitchell, 1992.

Classic One-Liners, by Gene Perret, 1992.

Heart, Humor & Healing, by Patty Wooten, 1994.

Joke Books

Treasury of Clean Church Jokes, by Tal Bonham, 1981.

Treasury of Clean Jokes, by Tal Bonham, 1981.

Treasury of Teenage Jokes, by Tal Bonham, 1986.

Treasury of Children's Jokes, by Tal Bonham, 1987.

Treasury of Senior Adult Jokes, by Tal Bonham, 1989.

Jokes for Children, by Marguerite Kohl, 1989.

500 More Hilarious Jokes for Kids, by Jeff Rovin, 1990.

The Official Smart Kids/Dumb Parents Joke Book, by Larry Wilde, 1977.

Humor, Health and Happiness

Anatomy of an Illness, by Norman Cousins, 1979.

Head First—the Biology of Hope, by Norman Cousins, 1989.

Healing Power of Humor, by Allen Klein, 1989.

Being Happy, by Andrew Matthews, 1990.

The Joyful Christ, by Cal Samra, 1986.

Peace, Love and Healing, by Bernie Siegel, 1990.

Humorous Videos

Abbott and Costello Meet Frankenstein

Airplane

All of Me

Best of Candid Camera: Special Edition

Best of Soupy Sales Shows

Bill Cosby - Himself

Blazing Saddles

Buster Keaton - any film

Charlie Chaplin - any film

Classic Comedy Teams

Honeymooners

It's a Mad, Mad, Mad World

Life and Depth - Joe Kogel

Marx Brothers - Duck Soup

Naked Gun

Return of the Pink Panther

Robin Williams - Live at the Met

Shirley Temple films

Sid Caesar's - Ten from Your Show of Shows

Some Like It Hot

Steel Magnolias

Take the Money and Run

The Gods Must Be Crazy

The Jerk

Uncle Buck

Hospital Humor Programs (partial list)

Albert Einstein Medical Center
    5501 Old York Rd., Philadelphia, PA 19141

Baptist East Hospital
    4000 Kresge Way, Louisville, KY 40207-4676

Columbia Presbyterian Med. Center
    622 W 168th St., New York, NY 10032-3796

Naples Community Hospital
   350 7th St., North Naples, FL 33940-5791
Copley Hospital
   RD 3, Box 760, Morrisville, VT 05661
Duke University Hospital
   Erwin Rd., Durham, NC 27710
Immanuel Medical Center
   6901 N. 72nd St., Omaha, NE 68122-1799
Ethel Percy Andres Gerontology Center
   LAC-USC Medical Center
   1200 N. State St., Los Angeles, CA 90033-1084
South Fulton Hospital
   1170 Cleveland Ave., East Point, GA 30344-3665
Highland Hospital of Rochester
   1000 South Ave., Rochester, NY 14620-2782
Humana Hospital of Overland Park
   10500 Quivira Rd., Box 15959, Overland Park, KS 66215-5959
Mesa Lutheran Hospital
   525 W Brown Rd., Mesa, AZ 85201-3299
Morton F. Plant Hospital
   323 Jeffords St., Box 210, Clearwater FL 34617-0210
Rice Memorial Hospital
   301 Becker Ave. SW, Willmar, MN 56201
Shawnee Mission Medical Center
   9100 W. 74th St., Box 2923, Shawnee Mission, KS 66201-1323
St. Francis Medical Center
   400 45th St., Pittsburg, PA 15201
St. Joseph Hospital
   1919 La Branch St., Houston, TX 77002-8399
St. Joseph's Hospital
   301 Prospect Ave., Syracuse, NY 13203-1895
St. Peter's Hospital
   315 S Manning Blvd., Albany, NY 12208-1789
Sunnyview Rehabilitation Hospital and Center
   1270 Belmont Ave., Schenectady, NY 12308-2198
Tuolumne General Hospital
   101 Hospital Rd., Sonora, CA 95370-5297

Harbor-UCLA Medical Center

    1000 W Carson St., Torrance, CA 90502-2069

University Hospital

    2211 Lomas Blvd. NE, Albuquerque, NM 87106-2745

University of Michigan Medical Center

    1500 E. Medical Center Dr., Ann Arbor, MI 48109

Veterans Administration Medical Center

    3495 Bailey Ave., Buffalo, NY 14215-1195

Caring Clown Programs (partial list)

Columbia Presbyterian Medical Center - Babies Hospital

    622 W. 168th St., New York, NY 10032-3796

Ottumwa Regional Health Center

    1001 Pennsylvania Ave., Ottumwa, IA 52501-2186

St. Charles Medical Center

    2500 NE Neff Rd., Bend, OR 97701-6098

St. James Hospital Clown Connection

    1423 Chicago Rd., Chicago Heights, IL 60411-3483

St. Luke's Methodist Hospital

    1026 A Ave NE, Box 3026, Cedar Rapids, IA 52406-5098

Speakers on Humor

Center for the Laughing Spirit - Lee Glickstein, 288 Juanita Way, San Francisco, CA 94127; Phone: (415) 731-6640, Fax: (415) 731-4213

Centre in Favour of Laughter - Dhyan Sutorius, Jupiter 1007, NL-115 TX, Duivendrecht, The Netherlands; Phone: 31-20-6900-289

Comedy Connection - Leslie Gibson, 1223 Dinnerbell Lane, Dunedin, FL 34698; Phone: (813) 733-9167

Gesundheit - Patch Adams, PO Box 2264, Wheeling, WV 26003; Phone: (304) 242-2048

Health and Humor Seminars - Dixie Schneider, 8085 Hans Engle Way, Ste. 100, Fair Oaks, CA 95628; Phone: (916) 965-7126, Fax: (916) 863-0378; Email: rxdixie@aol.com

HUMORx - Karyn Buxman, PO Box 1273, Hannibal, MO 63401; Phone or Fax: (314) 221-9086, Email: humorx@aol.com

Jane Hill - Keep Laughing to Keep Healthy - Jane Hill, 3941 So. "E" Bristol St., Suite 337, Santa Ana, CA 92704; Phone: (714) 546-2339

Jest for the Health of It - Patty Wooten, PO Box 4040, Davis, CA 95617; Phone: (916) 758-3826, Fax: (916) 753-7638, Email: jestpatty@aol.com

Jocularity Speakers Bureau - Free referral service for humor and health speakers Doug Fletcher, PO Box 40416, Mesa, AZ 85274; Phone: (602) 835-6165, Fax: (602) 835-6922, Email: laffinrn@neta.com

Jollytologist - Allen Klein, 1034 Page St., San Francisco, CA 94117; Phone: (415) 431-1913, Fax: (415) 431-8600, E-mail: allenklein@aol.com

Laughing Heart - Liz Curtis-Higgs, PO Box 43577, Louisville, KY 40253; Phone and Fax: (502) 254-5454

Laughing Matters - Donna Strickland, PO Box 18423, Denver, CO 80218; Phone: (303) 777-7997, Fax: (303) 777-1357, Email: stricklaff@aol.com

Laughter Centre - Chris Roberts, Badsley Moor Lane, Rotherham, UK S65 2QU

Laughter Clinic - Robert Holden, 34 Denewood Ave., Handsworth Wood, Birmingham, UK B20 2AB; Phone and Fax: 0121-551-2934

Laughter Remedy - Paul McGhee, 45 North Fullerton Ave., Montclair, NJ 07042; Phone and Fax: (201) 783-8383

Laughter Works Seminars - Jim Pelley, PO Box 1076, Fair Oaks, CA 95628; Phone and Fax: (916) 863-1592, Email: jimpelley@aol.com

Lighten Up Seriously - Sandy Ritz, 1532A Anuhea Pl., Honolulu, HI 96816; Phone and Fax: (808)737-4929

Making Humor Work - Terry Paulson, 28717 Colina Vista, Agoura Hills, CA 91301; Phone: (818) 991-5110, Fax: (818) 991-9648, E-mail: drterryp@aol.com

Mirthworks - Steve Kissell, 1227 Manchester Ave., Norfolk, VA 23508; Phone: (804) 423-3867

New Perspectives - Kathleen Passanisi, 9 Stone Falcon Ct., Lake St. Louis, MO 63367; Phone: (314) 561-2516, Fax: (314) 561-2520

Planet Mirth - Polly Schack, 5411 Pleasant St., Sacramento, CA 95822; Phone: (916) 444-6934, Email: pmirth@aol.com

Surprise, Inc. - Mark Darby, 2917 North 49th Street, Omaha, NE 68104; Phone: (402) 451-3459, Email: mdarby@gonix.com

Speakers About Compassion and
The Heart of Caring

Barbara and Larry Dossey - 878 Paseo Del Sur, Santa Fe, NM 87501;
  Phone: (505) 986-8188, Fax: (505) 986-1614

Center for Human Caring - Carol Montgomery, University of Colorado School of
  Nursing, 4200 E. 9th Ave., Denver, CO 80262; Phone: (303) 270-6157

Center for Nursing Excellence - Helene Nawrocki and Sandra Crandell,
  9 Maureen Road, #6, Holland, PA 18966; Phone: (215) 396-2510

Commune-A-Key Seminars - Caryn Summers, PO Box 58637, Salt Lake City, UT
  84158; Phone: (801) 581-9191, Fax: (801) 581-9196, Email: cakpublish@aol.com

Concepts of Care - Debra Townsend, 7706 N.W. Eastside Dr., Weatherby Lake, MO
  64152; Phone: (816) 587-5502

CPM Resources - Bonnie Wesorick, 100 Michigan N.E., Grand Rapids, MI 49503;
  Phone: (616) 776-2017, Fax: (616) 456-2770

International Association for Human Caring - Delores Gaut, 8680 S.W. Shetland
  Ct., Beaverton, OR 97005

Index

Bibliography

Adams, Patch & Maureen Mylander. *Gesundheit!* Rochester VT: Healing Arts Press, 1993.

Ader, Robert (Ed.). *Psychoneuroimmunology*. New York: Academic Press, 1991.

Arnold, Susan. "Jingle Bells." In London, F. (Ed.). *Whinorreha and Other Nursing Diagnoses*. Mesa, AZ: JNJ Publishing, 1995, 101.

Bain, Roly. *Fools Rush In*. London: Marshall Pickering, 1993.

Bartrop, R.W., Luckhurst, K., Lazarus, L., Kiloh, L.G., & Penny, R. "Depressed Lymphocyte Function After Bereavement." Lancet. (1), 1977, 834-839.

Bates, Roger. *How to be Funnier, Happier, Healthier and More Successful Too!* Minneapolis: Trafton Publishing, 1995.

Benner, P. & Wrubel, J. *Primacy of Caring*. Menlo Park CA: Addison-Wesley, 1989.

Berk, L.S., Tan, S.A., et al. "Humor Associated Laughter Decreases Cortisol and Increases Spontaneous Lymphocyte Blastogenesis." Clinical Research. (36), 1988, 435A.

Berk, L.S., Tan, S.A., et al. "Eustress of Mirthful Laughter Modifies Natural Killer Cell Activity." Clinical Research. (37), 1989a, 115A.

Berk, Lee & Tan, Stanley. "Neuroendocrine and Stress Hormone Changes During Mirthful Laughter." The American Journal of the Medical Sciences. 1989b, (298) 390-396.

Berk, L.S. & Tan, S.A. "Immune System Changes During Humor Associated with Laughter." Clinical Research. (39),1991, 124A.

Berk, L.S. & Tan, S.A. "Eustress of Humor Associated Laughter Modulates Specific Immune System Components." Annals of Behavioral Medicine. (15), 1993, S111.

Blalock, J.E. "The Immune System As a Sensory Organ." Journal of Immunology. (132), 1984, 1067-1070.

Blalock, J.E. "A Molecular Basis for Bidirectional Communication Between the Immune and Neuroendocrine Systems." Physiological Reviews. (69), 1989, 1-32.

Bombeck, Erma. *I Want to Grow Up, I Want to Grow Hair, I Want to Go to Boise*. New York: Harper & Row, 1989.

Bonhom, Tom. *Treasury of Clean Jokes*, Nashville: Broadman & Holman, 1981.

Bosker, Gideon. *Medicine's the Best Laughter*. St. Louis: Mosby, 1995

Brilliant, Ashleigh. *I Want to Reach Your Mind—Where is It Currently Located?* Santa Barbara CA: Woodbridge Press, 1994.

Brown, Joseph. "The Wisdom of the Contrary." In Parabola. 4 (1), 1979, 54-65.

Bruchac, Joseph. "Striking the Pole: American Indian Humor." In Parabola. 12 (4), 1987, 22-29.

Butler, Katherine. (Ed). *The Heart of Healing.* Turner Publishing, Inc.: Atlanta, 1993.

Buxman, Karyn. "Make Room for Laughter." <u>American Journal of Nursing</u>. December, 1991, 46-50.

Buxman, K. & LeMoine, A. (Eds.). *Nursing Perspectives on Humor.* Staten Island, NY: Power Publications, 1995. 125-132

Cannon, Walter. "Stresses and Strains of Homeostasis." <u>The American Journal of the Medical Sciences</u>. 189 (2), 1935.

Carter, Judy. *Stand Up Comedy.* New York: Dell Publishing, 1989.

Cline, Paul. *Fools, Clowns and Jesters.* LaJolla, CA: Green Tiger Press, 1983.

Cocker, John. *Best of Stitches.* Toronto: Stoddard, Inc., 1994.

Coffee, Gerald. *Beyond Survival.* New York: Putnum, 1990.

Cousins, Norman. *Anatomy of an Illness.* New York: W. W. Norton, 1979.

Cousins, Norman. *Head First—the Biology of Hope.* New York: Dutton, 1989.

Cushing, Frank. "Zuni Breadstuff." <u>Indian Notes and Monographs,</u> Vol. 8, New York: Heye Foundation, 1920.

Darrach, J. "Send in the Clowns—Clown Care Unit." LIFE Magazine, Aug., 1990, 76-85.

Dillon, Kathleen, & Minchoff, Brian. "Positive Emotional States and Enhancement of the Immune System." <u>International Journal of Psychiatry in Medicine</u>. 5 (1), 1986, 13-18.

Dohrenwend, B.S. and Dohrenwend, B.P. (Eds.). *Stressful Life Events: Their Nature and Effects.* New York: Wiley, 1974.

Dohrenwend, B.S. & Dohrenwend, B.P. (Eds.). *Stressful Life Events and Their Contexts.* New York: Prodist, 1981.

Dossey, Larry. *Healing Words.* San Francisco: Harper, 1993.

Dunn, Joseph (Ed.). "Humor in the Brain: What Happens When We Laugh— Interview with Peter Derks." <u>Humor and Health Journal</u>. 4 (5) 1995, 1-7.

Dunn, Joseph (Ed.). "Comedy and Spirituality—An Interview with Conrad Hyers." <u>Humor and Health Journal</u>. 5 (2), 1996, 3-10.

Ekman, Paul. "Expression and the Nature of Emotion," in Scherer, K. & Ekman, P., Eds. *Approaches to Emotion.* Hillsdale, NJ: Lawrence Erlbaum, 1984, 324-29.

Ellenbogen, Glenn. *The Directory of Humor Magazines and Humor Organizations in America and Canada.* 3rd Ed. New York: Wry-Bred Press, 1992.

Erasmus, D. *The Praise of Folly.* Translated by Hoyt Hopewell Hudson. Princeton, NJ: Princeton University Press, 1941.

Farberow, N.L. & Frederick, C.J. "Training Manual for Human Service Workers in Major Disasters." Washington DC: National Institute of Mental Health, 1978, Pub. No. (ADM) 90-538.

Farley, Venner. *Nurses Pull It Together To Make a Difference.* Staten Island, NY: Power Publications, 1995.

Felten, David, et al. "Noradrenergic and Peptidergic Innervation of Lymphoid Tissue." Journal of Immunology, (135), 1985, 755-762.

Fife, Bruce. *Creative Clowning.* Colorado Springs: Java Pub, 1988.

Findlater, R. *Joe Grimaldi: His Life and Theater.* 2nd. Ed. Cambridge: Cambridge University Press, 1978.

Fletcher, Doug. "A Humor Journal for Nurses." In Buxman, K. & LeMoine, A. (Eds.) *Nursing Perspectives on Humor.* Staten Island, NY: Power Publications, 1995. 125-132.

Fox, Matthew. *A Spirituality Named Compassion.* Minneapolis, MN: Winston Press, 1979.

Frankl, Viktor. *Man's Search For Meaning.* New York: Simon and Schuster, 1959.

Frey, William. *Crying: The Mystery of Tears.* New York: Harper-Row, 1985.

Fry, William. "Mirth and Oxygen Saturation of Peripheral Blood." Psychotherapy and Psychosomatics, (19), 1971, 76-84.

Fry, W.F. "Mirth and the Human Cardiovascular System." in Mindess & Turek (Eds.) *The Study of Humor.* 1979, Los Angeles, CA: Antioch U. Press.

Fry, W.F. "Laughter and Health." Encyclopedia Britanica, Medical & Health Annuals: Special Report. USA: Encyclopedia Britannica, 1984, 259-262.

Fry, William. "Humor, Physiology and the Aging Process." In Nahemow, Lucille, (Ed.) *Humor and Aging.* Orlando, FL: Academic Press, 1986, 81-98.

Gaut, Dolores and Leininger, Madeline. (Eds.) *Caring: The Compassionate Healer.* New York: National League For Nursing, 1991, Pub. No. 15-2401.

Gibran, Kahil. *The Prophet.* New York: Alfred A. Knopf Publisher, 1976.

Gibson, Leslie. "Carts, Baskets and Rooms." In Buxman, K. & LeMoine, A. (Eds.) *Nursing Perspectives on Humor.* Staten Island, NY: Power Publications, 1995, 113-124.

Goldberg, Andy. *Improv Comedy.* New York: Samuel French Trade, 1991.

Grant. "Letters to the Editor." Journal of Nursing Jocularity. 2 (1), 1991, 3.

Green, Lila. "Feeling Good: Humor in The Facility." Journal of Long Term Care Administration. Fall, 1990, 5-8.

Grotjahn, Martin. *Beyond Laughter: A Psychoanalytical Approach to Humor.* New York: Pitman, 1960.

Gullickson, Colleen. "Listening Beyond the Laughter." in Buxman, K. & LeMoine, A. (Eds.) *Nursing Perspectives on Humor.* Staten Island, NY: Power Publications, 1995, 19-25.

Hageseth, Christian. *A Laughing Place.* Fort Collins, CO: Berwick Publishers, 1988.

Hammer, Kathryn. *And How Are We Feeling Today?.* Chicago: Contemporary Books, Inc., 1993.

Hample, Stuart & Eric Marshall. *Children's Letters to God*. New York: Workman Publishing, 1991.

Hauptman, Don. *Cruel and Unusual Puns*. New York: Dell Publishing, 1988.

Helitzer, Melvin. *Comedy Writing Secrets*. Cincinnatti: Writer's Digest Books, 1987.

Henry, Janet. *Surviving the Cure*. Cleveland, OH: Cope, Inc., 1984.

Herth, Kaye. "Laughter: A Nursing RX." American Journal of Nursing. 84 (8), 1984, 991-992.

His Holiness the Dalai Lama with Daniel Goleman, et al. *Worlds in Harmony*. Berkeley: Parallax Press, 1992.

Holmes, Richard & Rahe, Thomas. "Social Readjustment Rating Scale" Journal of Psychosomatidc Research. 11, 1967, 213-218.

Hyers, Conrad. *The Comic Vision and the Christian Faith*. New York: Pilgrim Press, 1981.

Hyers, Conrad. *And God Created Laughter*. Louisville, KY: Westminster-John Knox Press, 1987.

Hyers, Conrad. *The Spirituality of Comedy*. New Brunswick, NJ: Transaction Press, 1996.

Irwin, Michael, et al. "Life Events, Depressive Symptoms, and Immune Function." American Journal of Psychiatry. 144 (4), 1987, 437-441.

Isen, Alice. "Positive Affect Facilitates Creative Problem Solving." Journal of Personality and Social Psychology. 52, 1987, 1122-1131.

Jaeger, Lowell. "Why Dogs Smell Each Others Butts." In Koller, J. (Ed.), *Coyote Journal*. Berkeley: Wingbow Press, 1982.

Johnson, Cathy. "The Humor Basket Project." In London, F., (Ed.) *Whinorrhea and Other Nursing Diagnoses*. Mesa, AZ: JNJ Publishing, Inc., 1995, 186-187.

Johnston, Wayne. "To the Ones Left Behind." American Journal of Nursing, Aug, 1985, 936.

Kelly, Emmett. *Clown*. New York: Prentice Hall, 1954.

Kelly, L.Y. *Dimensions Of Professional Nursing*. (4th Ed.), New York: MacMillan Publishing, 1981.

Kiecolt-Glaser, Janice, et al. "Modulation of Cellular Immunity in Medical Students." Journal of Behavioral Medicine. (9), 1986, 5-21.

Kiecolt-Glaser, Janice, et al. "Stress-Related Immune Suppression: Health Implications." Brain, Behavior and Immunity. (1), 1987a, 7-20.

Kiecolt-Glaser, Janice, et al. "Marital Quality, Marital Disruption, and Immune Function." Psychosomatic Medicine. (49), 1987b, 13-34.

Kiecolt-Glaser, Janice, et al. "Spousal Caregivers of Dementia Victims: Longitudinal Changes in Immunity and Health." Psychosomatic Medicine. (53), 1991, 345-362.

King, Jan. *Hormones from Hell: The Ultimate Woman's Humor Book*. Los Angeles, CA: CCC Publications, 1990.

Klein, Allen. *The Healing Power of Humor*. Los Angeles, CA: Tarcher, 1989.

Klein, Allen. *Quotations to Cheer You Up When the World is Getting You Down*. NY, NY: Sterling Publishing, 1991.

Kobasa, Susanna, et al. "Personality and Social Resources in Stress Resistance." Journal of Personality & Social Psychology. (45), 1983, 839-843.

Kornfield, Jack & Feldman, Christina. *Stories of the Spirit, Stories of the Heart*. San Francisco: Harper, 1991.

Kornfield, Jack. *A Path with Heart*. New York: Bantam Books, 1993.

Kramer, Marlene. *Reality Shock: Why Nurses Leave Nursing*. St. Louis: C.V. Mosby, 1974.

Kuby, Janis. *Immunology*. New York: W.H. Freeman and Company, 1994.

Lederer, Richard. *Anguished English*. Charleston, SC: Wyrick & Co., 1987.

Lederer, Richard. *Get Thee to a Punnery*. New York: Dell Publishing, 1991.

Leeming, David. "The Hodja." In Parabola. 4 (1), 1979, 84-89.

Lefcourt, Herbert & Martin, Rod. *Humor and Life Stress: Antidote to Adversity*. New York: Springer-Verlag, 1986.

Lefcourt, Herbert, et al. "Humor and Immune System Function." International Journal of Humor Research. (3), 1990, 305-321.

Leininger, Madeline. *Caring: An Essential Human Need*. Thorofare, NJ: C.B. Slack, 1981.

Levenson, R., Ekman, P., & Friesen, W. "Voluntary Facial Action Generates Emotion-Specific Autonomic Nervous System Activity," Psychophysiology. (27), 1990, 363-84.

Levy, S., et al. "Prognostic Risk Assessments in Primary Breast Cancer by Behavioral and Immunological Parameters." Health Psychology. (4), 1985, 99-113.

Lewis, Richard. "Infant Joy." Parabola. 12 (4), 1987, 48-57.

Lipman, Steve. *Laughter In Hell, The Use Of Humor During The Holocaust*. Northvale, NJ: Jason Aronson, 1991.

London, Fran (Ed.) *Whinorrhea and Other Nursing Diagnoses*. Mesa, AZ: JNJ Publishing, Inc., 1995.

MacLean, Paul. "Brain Evolution Relating to Family, Play, and the Separation Call," Archives of General Psychiatry. (42), 1985, 405-417.

Manning-Sanders, Ruth. *The English Circus*. London: Werner Laurie, 1952.

Martin, R. & Leftcourt, H. "Sense of Humor as a Moderator of the Relation Between Stressors and Moods." Journal of Personality and Social Psychology. (45), 1983, 1313-1324.

Martin, R. & Dobbin, J., et al. "Sense of Humor, Hassles, and Immunoglobulin A: Evidence for a Stress-Moderating Effect of Humor." International Journal of Psychiatry in Medicine. (18), 1988, 93-105.

Maslach, Christina. *Burnout—The Cost of Caring*. Englewood Cliffs, NJ: Prentice-Hall, 1982.

McCloskey, J. C. & Bulechek, G. M. (Eds.). *Nursing Interventions Classification.* St. Louis: Mosby, 1992.

McGhee, Paul. *Humor: Its Origin And Development.* San Francisco: Freeman, 1979.

McGhee, Paul. *How to Develop Your Sense of Humor: Life Skills for Boosting Resilience and Job Performance Under Stress..* Dubuque, IA: Kendall-Hunt Publishing, 1994.

Mickle, Steve & Rich Hillman. *Death Is - A Lighter Look at a Grave Situation.* Saratoga, CA: R & E Publishers, 1993.

Montgomery, Carol. *Healing through Communication.* Newbury Park: Sage Publications, 1993.

Moran, C. "Does The Use Of Humor As A Coping Strategy Effect Stresses Associated With Emergency Work?" International Journal Of Mass Emergencies And Disasters. 8 (3),1990, 361-377.

Nahemow, Lucille, et al. (Eds.). *Humor and Aging.* Orlando: Academic Press, 1986.

Nezu, Arthur, Nezu, Christine, & Blissett, Sonia. "Sense of Humor as a Moderator of the Relation Between Stressful Events and Psychological Distress: A Prospective Analysis." Journal of Personality and Social Psychology. 54 (3), 1988, 520-525.

Nisker, Wes. *Crazy Wisdom.* Berkeley: Ten Speed Press, 1990.

Nouwen, Henri. *Compassion.* New Haven, CT: Yale University Press, 1980.

O'Malley, Betty. *Levity for Longevity.* Sarasota Springs, NY: Humor Project, 1992a.

O'Malley, Betty. *Medical Mirth.* Sarasota Springs, NY: Humor Project, 1992b.

Palmblad, Jan. "Stress and Immunologic Competence—Studies in Man." In Ader, Robert (Ed.) *Psychoneuroimmunology.* New York: Academic Press, 1981, 229-257.

Pedersen, K.A. "Another Language." Nursing 87. 17 (7), 1987, 19.

Perret, Gene. *How to Write and Sell Your Sense of Humor.* Cinncinati, OH: Writer's Digest Books, 1982.

Perret, Gene. *Classic One-Liners.* Sterling Publications, 1992.

Pert, Candace, et al. "Neuropeptides and their Receptors: A Psychosomatic Network." Journal of Immunology. (135), 1985, 820s-826s.

Pert, C. "The Wisdom of the Receptors: Neuropeptides, The Emotions, and Bodymind." Advances. (3), 1986, 8-16.

Pipkin, Turk. *Be a Clown.* New York: Workman Publishing, 1989.

Plessner, H. *Laughing and Crying: A Study of the Limits of Human Behavior.* Evanston, IL: Northwestern University, 1970.

Radin, Paul. *The Trickster.* New York: Schocken Books, 1972.

Radner, Gilda. *It's Always Something.* New York: Simon & Schuster, 1989.

Ram Dass. *How Can I Help?* New York: Alfred A. Knopf, 1991.

Ritz, Sandy. "Survivor Humor and Disaster Nursing." In Buxman, K. & LeMoine, A.
    (Eds.). *Nursing Perspectives on Humor.* Staten Island, NY: Power Publications,
    1995, 197-216.

Robinson, Vera. *Humor and the Health Professions*, 2nd Ed., Thorofare, NJ: Slack
    Publishers, 1991.

Roitt, Ivan; Brostoff, Johnathan & Male, David. *Immunology.* 3rd Ed. St. Louis:
    Mosby, 1993.

Rosenberg, Lisa. "Sick, Black, and Gallows Humor Among Emergency Caregivers,
    or— Are We Having Any Fun Yet?" In Buxman, K. & LeMoine, A. (Eds.). *Nursing
    Perspectives on Humor.* Staten Island, NY: Power Publications, 1995, 39-50.

Saltzman, David. *The Jester Has Lost His Jingle.* Palos Verdes Estates: The Jester
    Co., Inc., 1995.

Samra, Cal. *The Joyful Christ.* San Francisco CA: Harper & Row, 1986.

Samra, Cal. *Holy Humor.* Portage, MI: Fellowship of Merry Christians, 1996.

Sapolsky, Robert. *Why Zebras Don't Get Ulcers.* New York: W.H. Freeman, 1994.

Schleifer, Steven. "Suppression of Lymphocyte Stimulation Following Bereavement."
    Journal of the American Medical Association. (250), 1983, 374-377.

Sekaquaptewa, Emory. "One More Smile for a Hopi Clown." In Parabola. 4 (1),
    1979, 6-9.

Selye, Hans. *The Stress of Life.* New York: McGraw-Hill, 1956.

Selye, Hans. *Stress without Distress.* New York: Signet, 1974.

Seuss, Dr. *You're Only Old Once!* New York: Random House, 1986.

Sexson, Linda. "Craftsman of Chaos." In Parabola. 4 (1), 1979, 24-33.

Shames, Karilee. *The Nightengale Conspiracy.* 2nd Ed., Montclair, NJ: Enlighten-
    ment Press, 1994.

Shem, Samuel. *House of God.* New York: Dell Publishing, 1978.

Sherman, James. *The Magic of Humor in Caregiving.* Golden Valley, MN: Pathway
    Books, 1995.

Siegel, Bernie. *Love, Medicine, and Miracles.* New York: Harper-Collins, 1986.

Snowberg, Richard. *The Caring Clown, Part I.* LaCrosse, WI: Visual Arts, 1992.

Snowberg, Richard. *The Caring Clowns, Part II.* La Crosse, WI: Visual Magic, 1996.

Solomon, George. "Emotional and Personality Factors in the Onset and Course of
    Autoimmune Disease, Particularly Rheumatoid Arthritis." In Ader, Robert (Ed.).
    Psychoneuroimmunology. New York: Academic Press, 1981, 159-182.

Solomon, George. "The Emerging Field of Psychoneuroimmunology." Advances. (2),
    1985, 11.

Soloman, George. "Psychoneuroimmunology: Interactions Between Central Nervous
    System and Immune System." Journal of Neuroscience Research. (18), 1987, 1-9.

Speaight, G. *The Book of Clowns*. New York: Macmillan Publishing, 1980.

Stevenson, M.C. "The Zuni Indians: Their Mythology, Esoteric Societies, and Ceremonies." In 23rd Annual Report of the Bureau of American Ethnology. Washington, DC: Government Printing Office, 1904.

Stolzenberg, Mark. *Clown for Circus & Stage*. New York: Sterling Publishing, 1981.

Stone, Arthur, et al. "Evidence that Secretory IgA is Associated with Daily Mood." Journal of Personality and Social Psychology. (52), 1987, 988-993.

Storlie, F. "Time Off." American Journal of Nursing. (65) 9, 1965, 240.

Summers, Caryn. *Caregiver, Caretaker*. SLC, UT: Commune-A-Key Publishing, 1992.

Tedlock, Barbara. "Boundaries of Belief." In Parabola. 4 (1), 1979, 70-77.

Tedlock, Dennis. *Finding the Center: Narrative Poetry of the Zuni Indians*. Lincoln: University of Nebraska Press, 1978.

Temoshok, Lydia & Dreher, Henry. *The Type-C Connection*. New York: Random House, 1992.

Towsen, John. *Clowns*. New York: Hawthorn Books, 1976.

Wagner, Jane. *Edith Ann—My Life So Far*. New York: Hyperion, 1994.

Wavy Gravy. *Something Good for a Change*. New York: St. Martin's Press, 1992.

West, Serene. *Daily Word*. Unity Village, MO: Unity Press, 1993.

Wettach, Adrian. *Grock: King of Clowns*. London: Methuen, 1957.

Wettach, Adrian. *Life's a Lark*. London: Benjamin Blom, 1969.

White, C. & Howse, E. "Managing Humor; When Is It Funny—And When Is It Not?" Nursing Management, 24 (4),1993, 80-92.

Wilde, Larry.*The Official Smart Kids/Dumb Parents Joke Book*. NY, NY: Pinnacle Books, 1977.

Wilson, Tom. *Ziggy's School of Hard Knocks*. Kansas City: Andrews & McMeel, 1990.

Wooten, Patty. "Does A Humor Workshop Effect Nurse Burn-Out?" Journal of Nursing Jocularity. 2 (2), 1992a, 42-43.

Wooten, Patty. "Humor as Therapy for Patient and Caregiver." in Bell, W. (Ed.) *Pulmonary Rehabilitation*. Philadelphia, PA: J.B. Lippincott, 1992b, 422-434.

Wooten, Patty. "Interview with Bill Fry." Journal of Nursing Jocularity. 4(2), 1994a, 46-47.

Wooten, Patty. "Interview with Vera Robinson." Journal of Nursing Jocularity. 4 (4), 1994b, 46-47.

Wooten, Patty, (Ed.) *Heart, Humor & Healing*. SLC, UT: Commune-A-Key Publishing, 1994c.

Wooten, Patty. "Interview with Sandy Ritz." Journal of Nursing Jocularity. 5 (1), 1995a, 45-46.

Wooten, Patty. "Interview with Terry Bennett." Journal of Nursing Jocularity. 5 (3),

1995b, 46-47.

Wooten, Patty. "Interview with Joanna Bull of Gilda's Club." <u>Journal of Nursing Jocuarity</u>. 5 (4), 1995c, 45-46.

Wooten, Patty. "Send in the Clowns." in London, F. (Ed.) *Whinorrhea and Other Nursing Diagnoses.* Mesa, AZ: JNJ Publishing, Inc., 1995, 188-192.

Wooten, Patty. "Humor: An Antidote for Stress." <u>Holistic Nursing Practice</u>. 10 (2), 1996, 49-56.

Ziv, A. "Using Humor to Develop Creative Thinking." In McGhee, P. & Chapman, A. (Eds.). *Humor and Children's Development: A Guide to Practical Applications.* New York: Haworth, 1989.

About the Author

Patty Wooten is a successful nurse, a dynamic speaker, and an hilarious clown! She began her nursing career in 1969 and has had clinical experience in critical care, hospice, and home health. Along the way, Patty found she could cope with the stress of nursing by using her sense of humor!

Patty created her first clown, Scruffy, in 1976. As her clown skills blossomed, Patty realized she could blend her love of nursing with her love of clowning. So she created her wacky character, "Nancy Nurse" and her whimsical counterpart, "Nurse Kindheart" with whom she amuses and educates health care professionals and lay caregivers the world over on the power of humor in healing.

Founder of *Jest for the Health of It!,* Patty lectures, consults and assists in developing therapeutic humor programs across the US, Canada and Europe. She is the current President of the American Association for Therapeutic Humor and the author of more than 25 professional articles about humor and health.

Patty's successful first book, *Heart, Humor & Healing,* is a light-hearted collection of quotes, quips and stories which promote health and healing in patients and caregivers. Patty is dedicated to helping caregivers maintain their sense of humor—both on and off the job. And along with Nancy Nurse and Nurse Kindheart, Patty helps her audiences learn, laugh and heal!!

You may contact Patty at:

Jest For The Health Of It!
P.O. Box 4040
Davis, CA 95617-4040
(916) 758-3826
(916) 753-7638 Fax
e-mail: jestpatty@aol.com

Commune-A-Key Publishing and Seminars

Commune-A-Key Publishing and Seminars was established in 1992. Our mission statement, "Communicating Keys to Growth and Empowerment," describes our effort to publish books that inspsire and promote personal growth and wellness. Our books and products provide powerful ways to care for, discover and heal ourselves and others.

Our audience includes health care professionals and counselors, caregivers, men, women, people interested in Native American traditions—anyone interested in personal growth, psychology, recovery and inspiration. We hope you enjoy this book! If you have any comments, questions, or would like to be on our mailing list for future products and seminars, please write or call us at the address and phone number below.

Ordering Information

Commune-A-Key Publishing has a variety of books and products, including other works by Patty Wooten, RN. For further information on our books and audio tapes, or if you would like to receive a catalog, please write or call us at the address and phone number listed below.

Our authors are also available for seminars, workshops and lectures. Please call our toll-free number for further information.

Commune-A-Key Publishing
P.O. Box 58637
Salt Lake City, UT 84158
•

1-800-983-0600